Faces of Humanity

18 Narrative Snapshots Capturing The Essence Of The Human Spirit

Nitya Rao

Qurate
quratebooks.com

Faces of Humanity
18 Narrative Snapshots Capturing The Essence Of The Human Spirit
Nitya Rao

Published in 2024

© Published by

Qurate
qauratebooks.com

Qurate Books Pvt. Ltd.
Goa 403523, India
www.quratebooks.com
Tel: 1800-210-6527, Email: info@quratebooks.com

ISBN: 978-93-58983-97-5

Dedication

To the Suchak family, whose legacy spans four generations, from Dr. N. V. Suchak to Oliver. My dear friends Anil and Abha, and their children Suraj and Saloni, Om and Aahana, Aparajita (Tui) and Nathan, Lucas and Oliver.

To my cherished friends Poonam Prasad and Dimple Mishra.

To Simarann Verma, my daughter, who has always stood by me and woven a cocoon of love and care around Maitili and me over the years – your support means the world to us.

To Rajesh and Raghav Verma for their unconditional love

About the Author

Nitya Rao is a seasoned writer, photographer, traveller and a social worker, whose diverse experiences have shaped a profound understanding of the human spirit.

Having witnessed the fabric of rural India and the struggles of the less fortunate, Nitya has dedicated significant efforts to social work, including serving in the aftermath of two major earthquakes in Uttarkashi and Bhuj.

His second book, **Faces of Humanity,** reflects the inner churning of his life's experiences, bridging the worlds of the privileged and the underprivileged. Through his vivid storytelling, Nitya captures the essence of pain, suffering, joy, and brotherhood, promising readers a journey that will inspire, uplift, and resonate deeply with their consciousness.

CONTENTS

INTRODUCTION

Dive into a mosaic of human experience with 'Faces of Humanity', a captivating collection of 18 short narratives that explore the breadth of life's emotions and complexities. From the quiet moments of introspection to the intense throes of passion, each tale illuminates a unique facet of the human condition. Meet characters whose lives intertwine with fate in unexpected ways, discover secrets hidden beneath everyday interactions, and journey through worlds both familiar and fantastical. Whether it's the thrill of first love, the pain of loss, or the joy of redemption, this anthology offers a poignant and thought-provoking glimpse into what it means to be human.

Perfect for readers seeking stories that resonate long after the final page is turned, 'Faces of Humanity' is a testament to the power of storytelling to connect us all.

CROOKED LINE

"Glance into the world just as though time were gone: and everything crooked will become straight to you."

-Friedrich Nietzsche

Sameera was a fun-loving girl before she married Nikhil. She accepted the proposal as he was an artist too. She later realised that his paintings were not in demand, due to which he became very frustrated and started to drink. Family burden and a drunkard husband took out all the fun out of her life. She had not signed up for this when she had got married. She took up a job and was very good at it as she was an artist. She was the bread winner of the family.

Nikhil's parents apologised to her. She told them that it was too late for it. She also reminded them that their gamble - he will change after marriage had boomeranged and also that as an artist, he couldn't draw a straight line because of which no one was interested in his art. One day when she met up with her childhood friend, she narrated her married life story. Her friend listened quietly and told her that she believed in Sameera's capabilities and abilities. Sameera reminded her that the problem was not her capabilities but the drinking of her husband.

Her friend then sent her a poem by an unknown author, 'Oyster'. She said that this was her answer. She read it over and over again to gain inspiration to change her husband but couldn't find a way. She took him to various alcohol anonymous centres. They assured her, that her husband would stop drinking but it never worked; all of them had failed her.

Soon she realised that she was pregnant. She was not sure to be happy or sad. One part of her told her that she would have to make more time. The other side of her was very happy. A child brings joy into the house. Since her marriage, there was no joy in the house. She hoped that the child's laughter would vibrate in the house and would change her husband. She delivered a healthy baby boy. She hired a kind old lady to look after her baby. There was no change in her husband. Only difference was that he now came late so as not to disturb the child who would be asleep.

One day, she received a call at around midnight. The call knocked her out completely. It was from the police to inform her that Nikhil had met with an accident. They asked her to come to the hospital. She rushed there only to hear that the accident was fatal and he had died on the spot. She rang up her friends, colleagues, relatives and neighbours to inform them. His funeral and last rites were conducted as directed by the elders of the family. She mentally took review of her life and knew that she had no one to fall back upon. Not that her husband was of much help.

She slowly started to plan her child's life. She became a very strict mother. Her aim was to make the child very bright and intelligent. She took up painting at home as it provided her extra income as well as it gave her profound satisfaction. She always told her near and dear ones that painting liberated her soul. Her paintings reflected joy and happiness. People in her paintings were full of laughter and joy. It reflected her childhood.

When her son Sanil was two years old, she started to teach him how to draw. He was not able to grasp drawings, as it reminded him of the drunken father and an upset mother fighting. His memory of his father not drawing as good as his mother and she taunting him for that, hurt him. He never wanted to take up drawing and hence, he never ever drew a straight line. This upset her very much as she dreamt of making him a child prodigy.

She put a lot of pressure on the child regarding drawing, but nothing worked. She refused to accept that her son Sanil was not an artist. The old lady tried to explain to her that each child has different natural abilities. She needs to find out what is that one skill Sanil is born with. This only angered her very much. She accused the old lady of diverting the small child's mind into other things. Since the old lady was with the child most of his waking hours, she knew his liking but could not express it, as it would upset Sameera.

The old lady had observed that since childhood, Sanil was attracted to music. If he would hear music from some distant loudspeaker or radio, he would run towards the window to try to hear it clearly. He would also shake his head and hand to the rhythm or beat. The old lady had once tried to draw Sameera's attention to it. She was admonished saying that she should not encourage nor put such things in the innocent child's mind!

Sanil started to go to the nursery. He did very well there in all activities apart from drawing. During the parent-teacher meeting, she was told about it. That's why she took it upon herself to teach Sanil drawing. His drawings were either tilted upwards or downwards. It was never straight. He seemed to lack the ability to draw a straight line.

After a few years, he was now in third standard. Sameera's paintings were selling well, her income from sales of paintings was more than adequate, so she left her job and was now full time at home. Sanil would meet her in the study room before going to school and after coming back from school. If she was a little free, she would make him draw. She used to get frustrated from the fact that he couldn't draw a straight line! She had learned to control her anger and frustration.

One day, she was sitting by the open window to gain inspiration from nature. That window had a very good view of the distant mountain and green forest. It was her go-to place, not only for inspiration but peace and even clearing her mind. Though life was running smoothly outside, she was not in a good place inside. There was frustration and anger over her life after the marriage. She didn't know whom to blame as the one whom she always blamed was no more. That's why the view from this window brought her peace and solace.

Previously, Sameera had been stubborn about teaching Sanil to draw, frustrated by his inability to cope. Sanil, feeling responsible for his mother's frustration, had tried ways to train himself to draw straight lines to impress his mother. He started learning riding his bicycle straight. It was during one of these attempts that he accidentally fell and banged his head on a stone. Sameera realised that her insistence had pushed him to this dangerous path.

Panicked, she rushed to Sanil, finding him bleeding. She picked him up and hurried to the nearby hospital's emergency ward. The doctors quickly took him to the ICU, connecting him to various machines and attending to his injuries. Sameera stood at a distance, devastated, watching the doctors work. Sanil was put on a ventilator, and she anxiously watched the monitor displaying his pulse and oxygen levels. As his breathing became laboured, the readings started to drop, and the waves on the monitor grew smaller. The doctors began to pump his chest in an effort to save him.

In the ICU, he suddenly was sinking and the significance of the straight line on the heart rate monitor became clear to Sameera. That straight line signified death! She looked at the monitor in those critical moments and shouted, "No straight line, please! Please don't make a straight line. I will never force you ever to make one!"

A nurse came and pulled her back. The doctor once again pumped Sanil's chest. Sanil let out a loud grunt. Hearing that, Sameera collapsed in the nurse's hand. When she gained consciousness, she learnt that Sanil was safe. His head injury was bad but he would recover from it.

The only thought that passed through her was her promise that henceforth she would never ever force him to draw a straight line!

FLAG

"Either I will come back after hoisting the Tricolor, or I will come back wrapped in it, but I will be back for sure."

- Captain Vikram Batra

Brigadier Amar Singh was posted in Mumbai after a span of 10 years. It was home coming for him and his family. Born and brought up in this city, he opted for it before his retirement in six months. His planning was perfect. He purchased a house and moved in during the service as he knew that it would be easy for the family to get settled. Children had already come early to set things up for them. News of border skirmish regularly trickled in. But Mumbai being far away from the border action, his family was never worried.

They all were settling down to live a normal life. Brigadier would go in the morning and would be back by evening. Sometimes he would go to the club for meeting colleagues and friends.

One day, Brigadier was back by afternoon and with him accompanied two jawans. He informed that his battalion has been called near the border. There had been new developments there. That was all he could reveal. He quickly packed and the jawans picked up the luggage. Brigadier hugged everyone and left.

Brigadier Amar Singh's posting was in Uri sector. The first work was to tap all local sources. Having activated them, the next task was to gather intel.

Lots of loose talks kept floating around as some of the sources were double agents. They would give wrong intel! The army would gather information from all sources and then analyse them, filtering the wrong ones before coming into any conclusion. Errors usually happened when the intel came in real time. Scope of counter-checking such real time intel was nil. At such times the personal on the field had to take the decision on the spot.

Brigadier Amar Singh lost three of his men in an ambush. The source was killed too.

There were strong rumours floating around, of this massive ambush. No one knew any more details of the area or dates of the attack. Hence, patrolling was tightened. Everyone was put on high alert. Suddenly there was a news that three terrorists had taken shelter in an abandoned building. The building was strategically built. All four sides had open space. So, forcing entry was next to impossible. Even entering in the night was dangerous as they may have night vision binoculars.

Brigadier Amar Singh requested for drones at night so that they could peep into the building and assess where the terrorists had placed themselves. Since only three terrorists were housed at any given time, one side was empty. The drones gave a clear picture of the terrorists. From the fourth side, the troops lined themselves on the wall of the building. By the time the terrorists changed position, the Army jawans had already surrounded them. It was just a matter of time. One of the drones had firing capabilities. To surprise them and ambush them it was used to injure one of the terrorists. The others came to see from where the bullet was fired. A drone was on purpose flown past them.

This diverting tactic paid off as the troops entered the building and killed two and captured the injured soldier. The Army was aware that there will be retaliation.

The next day the entire team was returning to the base when on an open sector a bomb laden jeep came and rammed into the jeep of Brigadier Amar Singh. Both vehicles blasted off in the air. Two terrorists, Brigadier, and his two aides all were blown to pieces.

News of the death of Brigadier Amar Singh was conveyed to the family. Few days later the same sepoy, who had come to take Brigadier, came with the bag and a flag. His son was very upset on seeing the sepoy. He charged at him and said, “You took my father away and returned back with a flag?”

FOOL

"A Fool can become a Genius when he understands he is a Fool. But, a Genius can become a Fool when he understands he is a Genius."

– Abdul Kalam

This is the story of Rahul who was considered a fool. He was actually a simpleton who did a lot of mistakes which made him look like a fool. He worked in a bakery. He loved experimenting without bothering of the result or consequences. One day, he poured a litre of oil on a loaf of bread to see if it would have the effect of a deep-fried bread. The loaf burst due to the heat and nearly burnt the bakery down. He was kicked out. His parents had died when he was young. His father's brother brought him up but had to throw him out of the house because of his experiments.

He worked in different fields and so he had little knowledge of everything but never mastered any one skill. His ability to grasp knowledge was never in question but his foolish idea of risking his and others' life and property put him in the bracket of fools. As the saying goes, "Fools rush where angels fear to tread." If the same thing would have been done in a controlled atmosphere taking all safety precautions, then one might have called it research!

Rahul then worked in a garage near the railway station. There was a continuous flow of people and vehicles. This kept him busy, so he had no time to experiment. The owner knew his flaws and hence asked everyone working to keep an eye on him.

One day, the city was rocked with series of bomb blasts at different locations. Most of them were carried by people and triggered by remote. The city police found a few that were time bombs.

The bomb squad was busy trying to defuse the bombs. This was the first of its kind in the city and hence the bomb defusing staff was less.

Outside the garage, there was a sudden commotion and people started screaming, "Run! Bomb. Bomb near the station! Run!" The owner immediately asked everyone to shut down and go. Rahul seemed unperturbed and was moving slowly, so the owner gave him the keys to shut the garage and ran away like others. The road was deserted, and Rahul ran towards the spot where the bomb was found. Police asked him to stay away but he went and studied it.

He brought two chairs and a box. He then went off to take the bomb out of the bag and place them on the two chairs. He then examined them from all sides. He knew he couldn't guess the wire, so he didn't attempt. He ran towards the garage and brought with him a long extension wire. He also had in his hand a drill machine. The police were very far away in the opposite direction of the garage. They yelled at him, but he cared less.

He lay on the floor on his back, in between the two chairs, with his head facing upwards towards the bomb. He held the edge of the bomb and started to drill; the most difficult manoeuvre in disposing a bomb. He drilled six holes and then with the help of a screwdriver and plyer he pulled the sheet. Gelatin sticks started to fall; some he took out with his hand. He got up and kicked the sticks away.

He was not sure if all had come out so he placed a box on the bomb and ran away as fast as he could. The time left was only one minute. He went and hid behind a parked car at a distance away. He crouched and waited. When the timer struck 00:00, the box placed above the bomb blew up high in the air. There was damage to the chairs. Probably one Gelatin stick was still inside it and hence the damage. A major disaster was averted.

A senior police officer commented, "The fool didn't think it was impossible. So, he did it."

This was the first time in his life he became a hero for his foolish experiment.

I AM HUNGRY

"We all have a hungry heart, and one of the things we hunger for is happiness. So as much as I possibly could, I stayed where I was happy."

-Mary Oliver

Bhiwandi is known for its textile industries. One of the largest power loom hubs in the state of Maharashtra. Mumbai housing sector boom and octroi issues gave birth to a new industry - warehousing. The lands which belonged to the local *Aagri's* were taken and huge godowns were built and rented. Bhiwandi has a large Muslim population. They too considered themselves locals. They too purchased land to start business.

The city traditionally respected people from all faiths. All festivals were celebrated in a peaceful and cordial manner. Very near the main bus stop there was an open space. Hutments slowly took over the open space. Two poor families built their huts adjacent to each other. One belonged to Shaikh Mohammed and the other to Shoban Singh. The families became very close to each other, like brothers. If any one family earned money, both families would share it together. It saved money and wood. Wood was not easily available in the city. Their bond grew along with their difficulties. The boom only brought more people from around Maharashtra and other states.

The bonding of Mohammed and Shoban was a great example but none of the social workers ever got to know about it. Children were given free education. There was a lady who came to teach the children after her working hours. This helped the children a lot. She even taught hygiene and health care. Diarrhea was the common and most prevalent in the hutments.

Children ate from wherever they could and drank dirty water on a regular basis. Even though the teacher taught them not to, they had no option. Leftovers from the passengers on the bus stand were their only treat. At home, food was limited and many mouths to feed. Children were perpetually hungry. The only source of food was the leftovers. Some passengers even gave packed stale food of their homes. Very rarely did they get fresh food.

If someone felt philanthropic then he would buy fresh cooked food for them from the nearby food stall. The children considered that day their Eid and Diwali. Few years passed and more members in their families got added. The share of each member only reduced. Sleeping space too was compromised. One had to sleep in crouching positions. Each child started to feel the frustration.

News of riots in various parts of the state trickled in frequently. WhatsApp images and videos only added fuel to the fire. Elders from both communities met to think out a peaceful solution to the issue. Youngsters from both communities wanted to teach the other community a lesson. Political parties fuelled the fire by declaring a *bandh*. This way, each community knew that the other community would be at home.

Rumours were on the rampage and so were the youngsters from both communities. Initially the targets were other community from their area. Later it spread to the whole city. Wherever the police intervened they were made targets. Hence, the police were helpless bystanders. The mob was too large to control. Every day, someone or the other was killed in the lane in which Mohammed and Shoban lived. It was their friendship that saved both the families.

Whenever one community persons came to kill, either Shoban or Mohammed would come out and assure the rioters that his family is in the house. One day only a few of them came silently. The children were sitting outside and froze. One of them tried to warn but the rioters had reached their hut. One of the rioters asked, "Are you a Hindu or a Muslim?" One of the children innocently replied, "We are hungry." This melted the heart of the rioters, and they offered the loot of eatables to the children and left.

BOOKS

"Reading should not be presented to children as a chore, a duty. It should be offered as a gift."

- Kate DiCamillo

There is an imposition of lockdown in the city, and it is shut down completely. I am Laxmi and I live very near to the school and since the lockdown, the books are just lying in our house. My mother used to clean utensils, but she can't go as the transportation has come to a standstill. My dad too can't go to work as the shops are all closed. Luckily, some NGO had come in our area and supplied food to us twice a day. Some individuals have distributed biscuits and toffees to us.

I heard that in the road behind our home, no one has come there and one uncle died due to starvation. The situation is very bad in the city as lots of people have died. We can continuously hear the sirens of the Ambulance. Every time an Ambulance passes, my heart sinks and I feel very bad. I start to wonder if the patient will live or die. Such has been the impact of this Pandemic.

Suddenly out of the blue, a news came that the lockdown would be lifted. I was happy and started to dust my books. Then I learnt that the schools are not starting but only the shops and offices are allowed to function with restricted hours only. Slowly all my enthusiasm died down. Boredom set in but along with that, issues of daily bread cropped up. Since shops opened up, the NGO stopped giving us food. Without any income source how can we buy the items for food? After much cajoling, one social worker agreed to arrange food for all of us in our lane.

Stocks being limited, the quantity was rationed. Something is always better than nothing and so we adjusted. Neither the NGOs nor the Government ever planned for people like us. We are always left to fend for ourselves. I heard stories of some youngsters forming a gang to rob the shops when they were shut. They did not have food for more than three days; hence they were forced to take up this action to save themselves as well as their loved ones. Restaurants, shops and offices were running at fifty percent capacity.

A month or two after the restrictions were finally relaxed, it was announced that the schools would restart. People were happy that they could once again see children running around in school uniforms. I once again took up the task of dusting and thoroughly cleaning up books and keeping it ready. One day before the school started, I picked up the books in my hand and went and waited for the signal to turn red. As soon as the signal turned red, I ran to the first car as I saw a lady sitting in it. I enquired if she would buy the book for her children.

I sell books at the signal to provide that extra income for me and my family. Even though I can't read and write I describe effectively what's written in the book because I have by hearted the contents to impress my clients.

OCEAN

"We must develop and maintain the capacity to forgive. He who is devoid of the power to forgive is devoid of the power to love. There is some good in the worst of us and some evil in the best of us. When we discover this, we are less prone to hate our enemies."

-Martin Luther King Jr.

Ranjeet and Chetna met during the Ganapati Festival. Chetna strayed away from her group due to the rush. Chetna was five feet five inches and hence could not see her group. She was jumping and trying to see them. Ranjeet saw this and offered to help. He held her hand and cut through the crowd. They were nowhere to be seen, as Chetna couldn't see them. Ranjeet asked Chetna to stand in front of him.

She looked with puzzled eyes towards him. He assured her, "Please trust me. What I will do is for your own good!" She had no choice, so she obeyed. He caught both her thighs and lifted her. In her shock Chetna was going to lose her balance backwards and bring both down. Ranjeet asked her to hold his head for support, which she did. She steadied herself and started to look around. She couldn't see her friends. Ranjeet asked her, "Spotted anyone?"

She replied, "No." He turned one quarter the other side and asked, "Now?" She replied, "Not yet." He again turned another quarter and asked, "Any luck?" Chetna in a disappointed tone said, "Nope." Ranjeet again turned another quarter and asked, "Can you spot anyone?" She in a sad tone said, "No!"

Ranjeet put her down and was short of breath. He gestured her to wait as he was catching his breath. She took out a bottle of water and offered it to him, saying, "This will help. Sorry because of me."

Ranjeet interrupted by saying, "No please don't say that." He then caught her hand and pulled her towards the divider of the road and said, "I think you should have the best view from up here."

Chetna exclaimed, "It is too high! I can't climb." Ranjeet smiled and said, "Like I told you, trust me." Ranjeet and Chetna reached the wall and again Ranjeet lifted Chetna. She climbed up and waited for him to climb up. She looked around but couldn't see anyone.

She scanned the whole crowd. She stood disappointed. Ranjeet suggested that check at the back. Ranjeet turned too and started scanning people when he spotted his school friend Prashant whom he called Barkya. He whistled and Prashant saw him. They both waved at each other. Just then Chetna spotted her friends and waved. The whole gang waved back excitingly.

Chetna started to wonder, "How come this guy whom I just met knows my friends?" She asked him, "How do you know them?"

Ranjeet said, "I know only Barkya, sorry Prashant. We are school friends."

She smiled and said, "For a second I thought were are a stalker! Such a small world."

Ranjeet jokingly said, "That is why the world is round. We keep meeting people. Sometimes again and again."

The gang came and Ranjeet and Chetna were formally introduced. Someone commented, "How were you'll were standing together when you'll don't even know each other?"

Ranjeet replied, "I just wanted to help her. I didn't ask her name, nor did she ask mine."

Prashant asked him, "With whom have you come?"

Ranjeet replied, "I came alone!"

Someone commented, "How convenient!"

Prashant asked others, "Do we add him in our group?"

Everyone agreed; that's how Ranjeet joined Prashant and Chetna's gang. Ranjeet got in touch with Chetna on a regular basis. They had a lot of things in common. Slowly, they fell in love. Ranjeet used to tease Chetna, "When I lifted you, that is the time I realized that I will have to lift you all my life! Trust me, Bappa was kind, and our meeting was his blessing!"

Chetna agreed, "Yes! No one could have planned such a meeting. It is blessings indeed!"

He took Chetna home and introduced her to his parents. They were pleased meeting Chetna who was down to earth and homely kind of person. Now it was time for him to go and meet Chetna's parents. Ranjeet was nervous and wondered whether they will accept him or not. Chetna had prepared her parents, so he did not have any trouble.

Everything went smoothly. Their parents met each other and fixed the date of their marriage. The wedding ceremony went off very well. Their gang was with them. Few members came with their family. After returning from their honeymoon, Chetna blended well in Ranjeet's family.

They were eager to have a child by the end of the first year! They consulted a doctor who said that both were perfect, but timing seemed to be a bit off; they should have patience. But Chetna was desperate for a child. Relatives, friends and neighbours put a lot of pressure on them.

One day, in June, Lord Ganapati visited Chetna in her dream and blessed both of them. Ranjeet's parents said that this is a sign.

In August they brought Ganapati home for Ganesh Chaturti. Ranjeet and Chetna decided that they will keep Ganapati for twelve days; one day extra than the prescribed eleven days which everyone keeps. They stayed a few hundred meters from the sea and hence it was very convenient.

In September, Chetna was pregnant and their belief in Ganapati's blessings only increased.

The next year of Ganapati celebration was grand with the arrival of their baby boy. As a tribute and gratitude, they named their child Ganesh.

Both Ranjeet and Chetna were doing well in their respective jobs. Little Ganesh was growing up and joined preschool. It was a very happy family. Ganesh finished his preschool and joined school in class Junior KG. Ganapati puja festival arrived and so did Ganapati arrive in their home.

Things didn't work out as planned. First time in years, Chetna missed the first two days of the puja due to her periods. As usual, they took it in their stride and moved on.

Except close relatives and friends, no one came to know. Duties were realloted and there was no slack in the festivities. This year, the murti was heavier as they had opted for the ecofriendly mud one. On the twelfth day they performed the last puja at home and took Ganapati in their car up to the seafront. On a cement block the placed Ganapati. The final puja was performed, and Ranjeet held the murti. Chetna held his hand as this year there was low tide.

They had to go deep into the sea about half a kilometre inside. As they bent to offer Ganapati to the sea as per the ritual, a wave emerged, and their legs got stuck up in the sand beneath. Ranjeet was busy trying to push Ganapati deeper into the sea. He did not notice that Chetna had fallen and was struggling to get up. In her fear, she became speechless and could not call out to him. As the wave receded back, it pulled Chetna along with it!

By the time Ranjeet realized, she had begun drifting away from him. His quickly held her hand and tried to pull her towards him, but the pull of the wave sucked him too! His parents were shouting for help but to no avail, as the sea had swallowed both of them. Police was called and fishermen were requested to help in the search operation. Ranjeet's parents were asked to go home with little Ganesh.

Next day, the bodies were recovered from the sea. They were sent for postmortem. The parents were given the body by evening.

The cremation and other rituals were performed. Ganesh was very disturbed and did not speak much to anyone. He preferred being alone. Understanding his circumstances, his grandparents left him alone.

One day, he requested his grandfather to take him to the beach near their house. On reaching the beach he stood straight and stiff very near the water. A wave came and lapped his feet. There were tears and angst in his eyes. The wave kept coming and lapping his feet. This went on for quite some time. Ganesh suddenly said, "Even if you touch my feet a thousand times, I won't forgive you for taking my parents away!"

COINS

"Coins always make sounds... But paper moneys are always silent. So, when your value increases, keep yourself silent and humble."

-Anonymous

Avinash lived on the streets, in a small hut built by his father. This was their third house. They were happy because his father got daily wages, while his mother got a monthly salary. They did not have much but they had enough to fill their bellies every day. Avinash went to the municipal school. He was good at studies due to the help of his uncle, Vithal who took tuitions. Vithal helped Avinash understand various aspects of life. Vithal always told him that one day Avinash will have a house in a building.

The reason of pressuring Avinash to excel in studies was so that he could do well in life. Vithal not only taught him academics but life lessons too. Vithal used to allow him to play sports only if the boys were good. Vithal always said, "Man is known by the company he keeps. So always have good people and good habits. That takes you far ahead in life." Whenever the first rain pours, Vithal would call Avinash and ask him to play in the rain. Vithal's belief was that if one gets wet in the first rain one does not catch any cold or water borne diseases prevalent in rainy season.

One day Avinash asked him, "Why are these people running towards the shelter?" Vithal replied, "The ones who have coins in their pocket enjoy the rain, whereas the ones who have notes run for shelter!"

The Government allowed everyone to have a bank account. His parents opened a joint account in their name. Vithal too opened one but insisted that one bank account to be opened in Avinash's name. Because of the persistence of Vithal, Avinash's bank account was opened.

When Avinash reached eighth standard, he started to do odd jobs under the guidance of Vithal. The entire earnings went into the bank account. Every weekend and holiday, some odd job was kept ready for Avinash. He never got to see his earnings nor his savings. Avinash, in the tenth standard made it in the merit list. Hence, he got scholarship to go to college. He purchased second-hand books from his savings account. He never stopped doing odd jobs.

He now earned a good amount as he was good at what he did. He did a job every evening at a nearby garage. The money was not much but he learnt a lot about the field. Whenever there was no class, he would rush to the library to learn all about cars. This way, he had the practical as well as the technical knowledge simultaneously. The garage worker and owner were very proud of him and hence if any client talked technical, they would ask him to answer the questions. He handled such clients very well.

Avinash finished his graduation and started applying for a real job. He preferred working around cars- its sales, its servicing etc. In one car sales and service centre, there was an opening for a clerk. Avinash thought something is better than nothing, so he applied. He was selected and joined in a week. He had only one set of clothes and he realized that if he has to work then he needs at least two more sets, which he purchased from his savings.

The first month he had to maintain the purchase inventory of the garage. A senior told him that if did not understand the spare parts Avinash could ask him. Avinash smiled but did not say anything. They thought he had good grasping power and hence he knew most of the items by name and its category. Few months passed; his supervisor noticed that he whenever they asked him to go the garage he would take his own time.

Also, whenever he was free too, he would go to the garage. To see what he does at the garage, the supervisor sent him on an errand. From the window he observed that the errand was over in a short time. Then he observed that the workers of the garage called him. He saw that they began briefing Avinash about a car. This puzzled the supervisor and when Avinash returned, he asked, "What were you doing in the garage?"

Avinash honestly replied, "Since they know that I like to learn about cars, they were showing me the new model that arrived recently."

One day, a client was enquiring the technical details of a particular car so the salesperson rang up for the garage supervisor only to know that he was absent. He briefed the others on the situation, and someone suggested, "Please contact Avinash in the office he will be able to help." The salesperson was desperate, so he called Avinash. Avinash met the client, and they discussed the technical aspects of the car.

Avinash had answers to all the questions of the client. A stunned salesperson was looking at Avinash with awe. The salesperson developed a sense of respect for Avinash. He was further shocked when Avinash closed the deal. The manager had got the news that there was an issue in the Sales Department so he came to see. He heard Avinash had convinced the client using his technical knowledge.

After the client left, the manager called both the salesperson and Avinash in his cabin. The salesperson briefed the manager the situation and why he had to call Avinash.

The manager asked Avinash, "You are working as a clerk in this company, isn't it?"

Avinash nodded in agreement. The manager continued, "Then how is that you know the technical details more than our salesperson?"

Avinash replied, "Sir, I worked in a garage for three years and repaired vehicles myself. Also, I am very interested in learning about cars, so during my off period in college, I used to go to the library and read all books available on cars. I also used to read at scrap merchants shop all the foreign magazines. This model is two and half year old. There has been more developments in the latest models abroad."

The salesperson said, "Sir, if you don't mind, I want to give a suggestion."

The manger nodded his head.

The salesperson continued, "As you are aware, we have a vacancy in the Sales Department. Why not transfer him into a sales role?"

The manger heard the suggestion and requested the salesperson to let him speak with Avinash in private. After the salesperson left, the manager asked Avinash to sit. The manager picked up the phone and called the HR person to come to his cabin. When the HR person arrived the manager ordered, "Prepare the necessary paperwork for Avinash's transfer from the Admin Department to the Sales Department. Please take him along with you."

The HR enquired, "Sir, as a trainee?"

The manager replied, "No as a regular employee."

In the appointment letter, Avinash learnt that his salary increased by fifty percent and plus he got other allowances. Avinash was very happy and went to the manager's cabin to thank him.

As soon as Avinash arrived, the manager said, "I was about to call and tell you that the client was so happy that he has ordered two more cars. Collect the details of the client and fill the sales form for two cars. This is your first sale! Congratulations!"

Avinash said, "Thank you Sir. Very kind of you."

The manager said, "You deserve it. Best wishes for a bright future in this new role!"

After duty hours, as he was heading home, he thought about his uncle, Vithal. His dream and vision had come true. In six months' time, he would be eligible to get house loan. He would have a house in a building!

As he was reaching the bus stop, it started to rain. He ran to find shelter. From the shelter, he saw three children dancing and playing in the rain. He smiled as his uncle's voice rang in his ears, "The ones who have coins in their pocket enjoy the rain, whereas the ones who have notes run for shelter." He realised he had journeyed from the coin to the note.

TRADITION

"The modernity of yesterday is the tradition of today, and the modernity of today will be tradition tomorrow."

-Jose Andres

Rathod Group of Industries was an internationally acclaimed business group. They owned several districts in India. Wherever they purchased land for their factory, they practically owned that district. This was their tradition. They had quite a few traditions like building hospitals, schools and colleges in those districts, for their employees and the local public. They were a highly respected family, and their employees were the loyal to them.

Many of the employees who worked there, were second to fifth generation workers. This loyalty had helped them maintain good quality products. They encouraged such employees in their factories and offices. Most of the employees' children's education came from the Rathod Trust. This helped them to keep a flock of loyal employees. The Managing Director, Shrichand Rathod became the youngest Director at the age of thirty. His father, Paramjeet Rathod had died in a road accident during one of his trips to Australia.

Shrichand was his only son and hence it was an easy transition. In fact, for the last ten generations, every newborn baby was a boy.

There was no girl child in the family line. Later, Shrichand's only son Vikram Rathod joined his family business. Shrichand and his wife, Urmila already started to plan for Vikram's marriage. They sent out a word in their family group to shortlist eligible girls.

Vikram saw few prospective girls but didn't find them compatible. His parents had filtered the list considering their family status and background. One day, Vikram returned home early as his meeting was in the same area and ended earlier than expected. He went to meet his mother in her room, but she was not there.

So, he waited in her room and knew that she would come. As he glanced around the room, he saw the file of prospective brides. He picked it up and glanced through it. He stopped at one page. He told himself that this girl seemed special. As he was ready to read her profile, his mother came. He bowed his head to her feet in the traditional manner. His mother noticed that one page of the file was open. She picked up the file, which he had kept on the table before bowing his head. She immediately said, "Your father and I have rejected this girl."

He enquired, "What is the reason for rejecting Gayatri, if I may ask?" Urmila replied, "In that family there are only girls no boys!"

Vikram was taken aback, "So what? Every family can't be like ours. Last ten generations we have had only boys! If everyone becomes like us, then we would have no girl to marry!" Saying that he gestured to his mother to hand him the file. Urmila handed him the file. He read the profile, and his face lit up.

He said, "I think this is the perfect girl. I request you'll to reconsider your decision. If you'll do so, I would like to meet her, before you'll talk to her parents." Saying this he left. Urmila informed Shrichand of Vikram's opinion. Shrichand asked for her profile. He quietly read it and said "I see why he liked her. I too think she will suit him perfectly. We will have to ignore the matter of no boys in their family."

This is the first time both disagreed on this topic. So, she started to read the profile without bias of no boys in her family.

She saw that this girl was intelligent and compassionate. She had volunteered for so many noble causes and put her heart and soul into it. The reason why both father and son liked her was that she had given talks on upholding traditions of family, state and business houses.

Urmila then arranged a meeting of Vikram and Gayatri at a resort. The idea was that it would be far away from the office, factory and home, hence the chances of anyone recognizing him was minimal. Special table was booked at the pool side.

Vikram had reached early as he was enthusiastic to see Gayatri in person. He had instructed everyone from the door keeper to the receptionist and the waiters to guide her to the table. This came naturally to him as he had arranged conferences as well as handled arrangements of delegates from abroad. He knew where the goof up takes place and hence, he instructed everyone so that if one person goofs up the other person will correct it.

Vikram shifted the chair arrangement so that he could see Gayatri when she arrived. Gayatri arrived and at that moment, the rays of the sun played with her hair making it look reddish black. He assumed that she must have used mehendi on her hair. She looked gorgeous and she wore a golden yellow top with frills. He observed that the colour suited her skin colour. Her face moved from sun to shade adding to her beauty.

He also noticed that she had spotted him but did not show it. Instead, she allowed the staff to guide her. He couldn't take his eyes off her but then feared it might not being polite. He started to see her gracious walk. It was purposeful and confident walk. She carried herself beautifully and gracefully. Whenever her hair threatened to come in the periphery of her vision she moved them away with a toss of her head. When Gayatri came near him, he stood up and shook her hands, which was soft as ever. He went around and pulled the chair for her.

She seemed impressed with his etiquette. He immediately told the waiter who had accompanied her, that they would order when they were ready. He watched the waiter go. Now he turned his undivided attention to Gayatri and formally introduced himself, "I am Vikram. Thank you for meeting me. I hope you had a pleasant ride." Gayatri smiled and said, "I am Gayatri. Thank you for inviting me. Yes, I had a pleasant ride. Hope your ride was pleasant too."

He said, "Yes thank you. You have a very impressive profile, and you are multi-talented. You are doing so many things at the same time. I am a fan of yours!" She did not blush, which indicated that she was used to receiving praises from strangers. She smiled and said, "Well thank you for your kind words. Your profile is interesting too. I learnt that you have gone abroad on business trips as well as held conferences of delegates from all over.

Since we both have done enough research on each other, I guess the only thing left is to talk about our personal likes and dislikes. Please tell me about yourself." He smiled and liked her approach, very practical he thought. He said, "Usually it's ladies first but since you have told me to start, I will abide by it. Let me start with my hobbies during my younger days. I loved photography, music, movies and sports to watch. I have played badminton, table tennis and cricket.

Not good enough to make it to my school team but in my division, I was among the top five. During the holidays, I used to travel to various places to understand the culture of the place and people. Nowadays, I travel only for business. I take a return flight immediately after the meeting. I never wait for anything except if there is a decision pending. I never topped my class but was good in academics.

I forgot to mention that I used to read a lot. I still do, but now it is more business related or if someone has recommended any particular book. Let me think what else about myself."

He paused briefly and continued, "I have never given a thought to this side of things myself as most of my relatives or friends know me by now." Gayatri interrupted by suggesting and enquiring, "Family, food, cuisines, habits?"

Vikram exclaimed, "Oh yes. Thanks. You must be aware that I am the only son of my parents. We have many relatives from father's side as well as my mother's side.

When we were small, during holidays we would get together or during any wedding. Nowadays all that has stopped as everyone is busy in their work. Wedding ceremonies are attended mainly by parents and elders. We are in touch once in a while. Food, I am not much fussy but love our traditional Marwadi food. Though I have eaten and tried all kinds of cuisines, I have never had a craving for them. I like platters and sizzlers.

I am a pure vegetarian, but I don't prefer Baingan, Karela and Doodhi. Having said that I don't mind eating Doodhi Halwa, though not often. Now to the last one you asked —habit. I like neat, tidy things and homes but personally I am not so good at them. Luckily, I have people to do it for me. I am not a hoarder, but I collect unique, exclusive and out of the ordinary things. I get angry at dishonesty, yet I am not always honest. Now, enough of myself! Now you may tell something about yourself. How do you define yourself?"

Gayatri smiled and said, "First of thank you for giving me a peek into you. You have very honestly answered and described yourself. There is clarity in your mind and the confidence that the listener will understand. I like the choices of your words.

You have interestingly asked about me. Well, after my college I joined my family business and also did some social work. I basically like helping people. Seeing my inclination towards social cause, my uncle suggested that I look after the CSR Department. I go to interior villages and at first hand see how they live and the difficulties they face in their day to day life. I don't believe in feeding them, but I love to make them self-sufficient. This being a very relative term one can't show the success of our work.

The CSR officials of our company say that as per the laws, we are to give a third-party impact assessment. For example, a person was having one chapatti earlier and after we helped him get on his own feet, he now eats 4 chapattis. For a city dweller, it is not seen as much of an impact. But for that person, it has made a huge difference! He is now getting many times more than what he had. Maybe ten years down the line, the difference will reflect distinctly. These are the challenges we have faced. Now I ask the third-party person to assess the condition and at the end of our project we ask him to reassess. This has solved most of our issues.

I love music, reading especially on spirituality and positivity. I am quite religious and as you might be aware that I love tradition in all its aspects. This is all about me. Let's order something before it becomes too late. I need to go too." Vikram smiled and asked her, "What would you like me to order for you?"

Gayatri said, "I will have toast sandwich and peach flavoured fresh lime juice."

Vikram said, "You have not even seen the menu." Gayatri interrupted saying, "If he doesn't have them, he will recommend. Why should I scan the menu card.?" She was giggling seeing Vikram's face.

Then she asked, "What would you like to eat or drink?"

Vikram gestured to the waiter and said, "I will taste your sandwich and have plain fresh lime juice." Gayatri teased him with a mischievous smile on her face, "How can you share from me? You have not even asked me. Moreover, you mentioned that you like Marwadi food so why not eat Kachori or something?" Saying this she started to giggle. Vikram too joined in by saying, "I will order two toast sandwiches. Half for me and one and half for you. Half extra is the punishment for not asking before assuming that I can share from yours."

Both were laughing and suddenly it struck Vikram that they were talking and behaving as if they knew each other. At this time, the waiter arrived. Before he could open his mouth Gayatri started ordering. She told the waiter, "One toast sandwich - crisp. One fresh lime juice and one Peach lime juice." Then asked Vikram, "Anything else you would like to order?"

He told the waiter, "Thank you, but that will be all."

As soon as the waiter left, Vikram told Gayatri, "You look lovely and the colour of this dress suits you."

She said, "Thank you, but don't you think you should have started with this?"

Vikram said, "I felt that if I started with this you might think that I am flirting. Now that we are comfortable with each other I thought you would understand."

Gayatri was in a mood of mischief. She said in a serious tone, "Don't get too comfortable I have not yet given my confirmation!"

Vikram saw through the mischief and said, "I know your answer and hence there is no need to say it aloud."

Gayatri continued, "So now you are a mind reader too?"

Vikram said, "No but a heart reader." He smiled and Gayatri lowered her eyelids as if hiding from him her real feelings.

Vikram then said, "When you laid your eyes on me and our eyes met, I knew your answer. That is why I told you in detail about myself. You too made me relax with your beautiful smile, warmth and acceptance. I know, you saw my love at first sight and hence you were totally relaxed. We both spoke as if we knew each other since ages!"

The waiter arrived with their order. They ate and sipped their drinks. Gayatri lightly slapped Vikram's hand and said, "You ate more than fifty percent of my sandwich." Vikram pretended as if his hand hurt. She smiled and said, "Stop acting. You are bad at it."

Vikram said, "I was trying to put your first touch in my memory bank."

This time, Gayatri blushed, and Vikram noticed it. He knew he had made a place in her heart as she had done in his. As they got up to leave Vikram locked his fingers in hers and walked her up to her car. After reaching the car he gave her a hug and said, "I'll be in touch. It was a very good evening. Time well spent." They both left in their respective cars.

Vikram and Gayatri's wedding was a grand celebration, worthy of the Rathod tradition and reputation. Attended by dignitaries, politicians, film stars and artists from every field. Being invited to the wedding itself was an honour. They went abroad for their honeymoon. After coming back, Gayatri remained at home as per Rathod tradition. Vikram was deep in his work. At night, Vikram would sit with Gayatri in the veranda and enjoy the cool breeze that was blowing. They talked on various subjects. Time was fleeting.

One day, the CSR Department got stuck with a problem of reporting. Shrichand called Vikram and said, "Sort out this matter and if need be, appoint a consultant. We don't want to be on the wrong side of the law."

Vikram said, "If you don't have any objections, then we can consult Gayatri. She has experience in this field."

Shrichand enquired, "Was it on her profile or did I hear it from someone?"

Vikram said, "Profile."

Shrichand said, "Yes okay, ask someone to send her all the files. Also ask the Department Chief to brief her on phone."

Vikram first briefed Gayatri and gave the necessary instructions. Urmila was surprised that files from the office were being sent home and that too for Gayatri. For the first-time, tradition was broken. No lady was ever consulted on office work nor was any file ever brought home!

Gayatri studied the file and made a list of suggestions and emailed it to Shrichand, Vikram and the CSR Department. At the end, she mentioned that if necessary, she was ready to be present in person to help. She mentioned that it would take not more than two days for its implementation.

Shrichand called a meeting of the CSR department at noon. It was decided that Gayatri would help implement the necessary changes. It was also decided that in all emails, Gayatri to be kept in cc and physical letters should be scanned and sent to her. When Urmila learnt of the new development, it shocked her. This girl is not only breaking traditions but trying to create new ones! She couldn't say anything as it was Shrichand's instructions.

One day, the good news that the entire Rathod family was waiting for, arrived. Gayatri was pregnant. Gayatri was the center of attention in the Rathod family. She was taken to their family gynaecologist by Urmila. Regular checkups were conducted, and

Urmila always accompanied her. After around twenty weeks, when Urmila and Gayatri had gone for the routine checkup during the Sonography, the doctor told Urmila that it was a girl.

Then the doctor instructed the nurse to give Gayatri an injection. The doctor explained that there was some complication in the pregnancy and hence they would need to sedate her. As Gayatri was losing consciousness, she was wheeled out of Sonography. When Gayatri became conscious, she was in the special ward. Urmila and the doctor were beside her. The doctor mentioned that the child had to be taken out as the umbilical cord had circled around the throat of the girl child. Urmila hugged Gayatri and informed that Shrichand and Vikram were on their way.

Gayatri was devastated and hugged Urmila tightly and howled in grief. She was uncontrollable, no amount of pacifying seemed to work. Just then, Vikram and Shrichand walked in. Vikram went and hugged Gayatri and started to cry. Both were crying and wiping each other's tears. Doctor told the nurse and then Urmila and Shrichand, "Let's wait outside. They need time with each other." Gayatri came into terms with her loss in a few weeks' time.

Vikram was very kind; he was there with her the whole time holding her in his arms and feeding her like a child. Later, he mentioned to her that his grief he could not address as he had to take care of her. He never cried as he would look weak in front of her. In a year's time, things were back to normal. In another six months, she got pregnant again.

This time too, same thing happened. This was too much for her to bear. She went to her parents' house for six months. Every weekend Vikram spent with her. Urmila was upset, as one more tradition was broken. The boy never stayed at his in laws house. She could not do anything as the situation was very delicate.

Two years later she was pregnant again. The same old story. This time, Gayatri knew something was fishy as she had gone a week ago to her mother's gynaecologist who had confirmed that no such threat was there. In the hospital she was alert and tried to study the nurses and staff. Vikram brought Gayatri home and both went to their room as she needed rest. As soon as they reached the room Gayatri asked Vikram to lock the door and put on the AC. Gayatri went to her cupboard and took out her older report and showed it to him.

Vikram was shocked and wanted to know who is behind this? Gayatri took out her mobile and played a recording of a senior staff who was retiring the next day. The lady revealed that, as soon as the scan shows it's a girl, Urmila signals to the doctor who then announces that there is a complication. Gayatri is given sleeping injection and wheeled to a room where surgical abortion is performed. She went on to mention that she heard her mother say that Urmila also suffered the same fate as Gayatri.

Vikram was shocked and angry. He got up when Gayatri held his hand. She told him, "If you really want to change this then please see that I get the permission to go to my house if I am pregnant again. If you ask me, I really don't want to get pregnant ever."

Both remained aloof and would only be with each other. One day, they were coming back from their walk and were passing their parents' room. They heard Shrichand telling Urmila, "This obsession of a male child has to stop! I told you so many times. These are today's children. In our times we did not know anything!"

Urmila intervened, "It's a tradition that has been going on for ten generations! I did not start it. I don't want to be one to stop it. I promised your mother on her last days that I will continue the tradition."

Vikram heard this. He barged into the bedroom and declared, "I will be the one who will stop this tradition. Gayatri will not promise you on your death bed. Remember this and also remember that you have blood of my children on your hands." Saying this Vikram stormed out of the room.

One and half year later, Gayatri was pregnant again. This time she went straight to her mother's house. Everything went of smoothly. On the day of the delivery, all were present except

Urmila. She did not want to see the face of a girl from her family. Gayatri delivered a healthy baby boy.

Gayatri held the child and looked up in the heavens and cried. "Sorry my three beautiful girls. You sacrificed yourself for him!"

She closed her eyes and saw three weeping girls. Later the staff came to see the boy. They were murmuring among themselves that the boy is so lucky to be born in such a rich family. Gayatri said to herself, "...at the cost of three girls weeping in heaven!".

FAMILIAR VOICE

"Sometimes, you just need that one phone call and that favourite voice to boost your soul."

-Anonymous

Rajan was studying BA and was in his final year. He was a simpleton by nature. He was not used to what the world did, to hide facts and speak white or grey lies. For Rajan, lie was a lie and truth a truth. It was either white or black; no grey areas in his life.

People would often take advantage of him. He would sometimes get beaten up too. He would defend by saying that he was a simpleton and not a fool. But very few people knew the difference between the two. He did not have true friends as people only wanted to take advantage of his nature. He didn't mind because helping others was his nature.

One day a girl, Mansi, approached him for help. He enquired the nature of the help she needed. She requested, "I come from a vernacular school and hence my English is not strong. If you don't mind, can you teach me English please?"

Rajan happily agreed. They decided that after college, they would sit in class if possible. On the first day, after the college lectures were over they sat in the class.

Ranjan commenced teaching, "The most important thing is that you should not get scared or feel shy when you speak English."

Mansi asked, "But how can I? I know that I make lots of mistakes!"

Rajan countered, "I don't want to behave like a teacher but please at least let me complete before you ask question."

Mansi giggled.

Rajan smiled, "I am happy that you have taken it in the right spirit. Where were we? Oh yes! Fear and shyness are two self-defeating attitudes."

Mansi raised her hand. Rajan nodded. Mansi asked, "What do you mean?"

Rajan elaborated, "Fear and shyness stop us from speaking. I agree there will be mistakes. If you don't speak, you don't learn. It is as simple as that. Now the question is, to whom should you start speaking with? Start with your parents, relatives or friends who will not laugh at you and most importantly will correct you. You can speak with me without any inhibitions, meaning, without fear and without feeling shy. The idea is to be comfortable in speaking. To improve your English, you can do somethings and it will help a lot."

Peon of the college came and interrupted, "Kids, you'll can't sit in the classroom after the class is over. I need to lock the room so please leave."

Both Rajan and Mansi got up and left.

As they were reaching the gate of the college Mansi asked, "Now where can we go?"

Rajan corrected her, saying, "Now where WILL we go?"

Mansi said, "Now decide."

Rajan thought for some time and suggested, "We can go to my house or yours. Which do you prefer?"

Mansi hesitated, "Will your parents like it? Will they say anything?"

Rajan replied, "I have never taken anyone home before, but I am sure they won't mind if I do."

Mansi looked surprised and added, "Really? That's nice. My parents will kill me!"

Few months went by, and Mansi's English improved a lot. She did well in her studies too. Like all youngsters, who get together for a long time they fell in love. Mansi was the one who expressed her feelings first. Rajan simply accepted it as he too liked her. They used to go together everywhere. Rajan's parents were happy with Mansi. One day, no one was in Rajan's house when Mansi and Rajan arrived.

Rajan took the keys from the neighbours and entered. He was teaching Mansi, but he noticed that her mind was not in it.

Rajan asked, "What's the matter? Why is your attention not in your studies? In fifteen days, we have our exams scheduled!"

Mansi placed her finger on his forehead and ran it down his face and chest and then said, "My sweet Rajan, how can you be so innocent?"

Rajan corrected, "Naive is the word you are looking for."

Mansi said, "Yes, naïve. Now stop correcting me and understand the feeling behind it! What a great opportunity has been provided to us and you are wasting it." Saying that she hugged him and started to kiss him.

He too responded and started to play with her and kiss her. When suddenly to his shock Mansi started to remove her clothes! He was totally dumbfounded. He was shivering and at the same in turmoil. He didn't know what to do or how to respond.

She tried to pull him towards her, but he excused himself to go to the washroom. Mansi was just buttoning up and cursed under her breath loudly enough for him to hear, "Impotent!"

The word pierced his heart like a sharp arrow.

He turned back and said, "It's that I don't want to do it before marriage."

She just left without speaking to him. He tried to speak to her, but she avoided him. He was torn from inside very badly. He thought that she loved him but then why was she not understanding? His mind kept asking himself.

He had no friends to share this with. He was bleeding inside. In the final exam, he just did average. His heart was madly in love with Mansi. He simply could not digest and accept her rejection.

After college, he joined his father's friend's firm. They were into servicing of water filters. He joined in the back office. He devoted his time and energy into his work. Nights were difficult.

His parents asked him to marry but he stalled it. After two and half years he was made a salesperson. His job was still back office but now he had a team of technicians under him. He also arranged for maintenance of units according to the schedule. He rang up clients and fixed time for maintenance.

He once rang up a client and a lady answered the phone. He said, "I rang up to ask for the time suitable for maintenance of the water purifier."

The lady on the other end replied, "Hello? I didn't understand!"

Rajan froze and staggeringly said, "Mansi? Rajan here."

Just then in the background he heard a man's voice saying, "Darling, whose call is it?"

The sweetest, loving and familiar to his ears voice said, "Wrong number!" and kept the phone down.

TOYS

"The relation between a child and a toy is like a relation of flower and its fragrance as both cannot be separated."

- Anonymous

Parikshit and Prerna and got married in a simple ceremony. Within a few years they were blessed with a daughter named Priti. She was a hyperactive child. For three years she got the undivided love from her parents and from her grandparents on both sides. She was a little princess, and everyone treated her like that. One day, a few years later, Prerna got pregnant again and Priti's world turned topsy-turvy. She was informed that she was going to have a brother or sister. Everyone now was eagerly awaiting the birth of the child.

All discussions were only on that topic. Little Priti felt sad and left out. Her parents started to see the change in her. They started to give her attention and time. They explained to her, that they were neither taking away nor sharing her love. They explained with an example to make her understand. They said, "You love both your parents and grandparents. Is one love greater than the other? Similarly, children too are both unique and share equal love!" On the scheduled day, a baby boy was born to the proud parents. Parikshit immediately placed the child on Priti's lap.

She was thrilled that she got the first chance to hold the baby boy. Pictures were taken of them together and of other family members. The whole house was filled with happiness and joy. Regular visitors came to see the mother and child. The boy was named Pankaj.

Six months later, Priti started going to school. She was busy and excited. Every day, after coming back from school she played with her brother.

Days flew fast and now it was time for Pankaj to start going to school. They both went together and came back together. Priti, being dominating by nature, was feared by all in school. Pankaj enjoyed this nature of Priti, as her reputation protected him from the bullies of his class.

Priti was now in secondary school and her dominating nature only increased every year. Pankaj got used to her nature of wanting all his things. Every toy of his would end up in her cupboard and only the ones that she didn't like or were broken were given to him to play. He played with only some of them, fearing that she would see them and take them away. He was glad that she was elder to him, otherwise his clothes too would have been worn by her!

He was always in fear, but he also knew that she loved him very much. So much so that one day she got scolded by their parents for protecting Pankaj. As is her nature, she fought for everything she loved.

When Pankaj for two or three days wasted food, parents decided that he needs to be reprimanded. They, in the heat of the moment raised their voice on Pankaj. Priti got very angry and shouted at them. She was punished for it but she didn't mind as she ended protecting him. She was inseparable from him, but she had her own rules in her head. Everything needed to be exactly as she conceived them.

One day, she came and dumped on the floor of his room, lots of toys. She noticed that he was playing with a new toy. This upset her no end. She took away the toy from him, stormed out of the room by slamming the door. Prerna — the mother, hearing the commotion came to his room in time to see Pankaj trip over one of the toys and fall on his back. His head hit the floor and a loud cracking sound filled the room. The colour of Prerna's face drained out.

She rushed into the room carefully and held Pankaj, who was bleeding badly. She rushed him to the nearby hospital. He remained critical for three days. On the fourth day, he succumbed to his injury!

Priti was very upset with everything that was happening but was helpless. The one person whom she loved the most, had gone out of her life. After all the rituals and condolences, she found herself alone. All these days she could not find the courage to go into Pankaj's room. She gathered herself and slowly entered his room. It had been tidied up by her mother. As was her habit, everything was in its place.

Priti sat on his bed and was still glancing around the room hoping he would just peep out of the cupboard or from behind the curtains as he used to do to tease her. He didn't come at all. Only tears rolled down her cheeks. She was devastated by the silence in the room. As she lifted her head, she glanced at his writing table. She wondered what he did the last time he was there. She sat on his chair and looked straight and found her picture stuck. This was a new one.

She recollected why the photo was taken. In her grief, she couldn't smile at her memory. She went on to look at the picture when she saw a bulge in one end of the picture. She touched it and realised that there was something under it. She slowly took off the edge of the picture and a paper fell down. She opened the paper and found that Pankaj had written a note for her. It read:

Dear Sis,

I love you very much and I am sorry to have kept a secret from you. It was a small victory for me. Hiding anything from you was impossible, so doing it for a year now (I will update it if you don't find it till then).

Behind and in-between my stack of clothes are hidden all new toys untouched even by me. It was tough as, Mom would come to clean the cupboard from time to time. The ones that I opened and played with are hidden behind my books. If you are reading this then I must have gone on some trip or to boarding.

I promised myself that if you find even one, I would have given you all. From today all the toys are yours. I know that you love playing with my toys. Enjoy them to your heart's content.

Your loving brother

Pankaj

KICK IN THE STOMACH

"A mother's joy begins when new life is stirring inside... when a tiny heartbeat is heard for the very first time, and a playful kick reminds her that she is never alone......"

- Anonymous

Aadhya fell in love with Advait and as their names were unique, they felt that their love was unique too. Two years had passed, and their courtship continued. They felt that now it was time to take their love to the next level. They both informed their respective parents. Aadhya's parents were thrilled whereas Advait's parents were upset. Advait thought he could make them understand. In the meanwhile, the courtship continued. Believing Advait, Aadhya continued the courtship. Advait assured her that he will make them understand and if they don't then he will abandon them for her. Such deep was their love and Advait's parents started putting pressure on him to discontinue his love life. He was clear and made it clear to his parents that he will marry Aadhya only. His younger sister Ivanka supported him in this matter. Days passed by and Advait and Aadhya started going out of town on weekends. They enjoyed each other's company. During one such weekend Advait did not have protection and yet they continued to have sex.

Parents gave up on Advait and started searching for a boy for Ivanka. Their search ended when they zeroed in on a boy who was working in Europe. His parents too liked Ivanka very much and had made up their mind. They said that their children both a boy and a girl will come down to India and after their approval only it will be finalised.

Ivanka's parents were happy for her and so was Advait. They were sure that the boy too would give his approval as Ivanka was a good smart girl. On a scheduled day, both children Seher and Shivani came to see Ivanka. Advait along with his parents were ready to receive them. Advait had made elaborate arrangements keeping in mind their likes and dislikes. After the formal introduction, Ivanka was asked to take Saher inside to speak and get to know each other.

Shivani was bored and so asked Advait to take her outside for fresh air. Advait obliged and spoke to Shivani enquiring about her life and her preferences. Shivani too enquired about his life and goals. He told her everything except about his love as he felt it didn't concern her. By the time they came back home they were quite friendly and comfortable with each other. Saher and Ivanka too had come to the living room and they too seemed comfortable with each other. Everyone was happy as the boy and girl agreed.

There were celebrations and lunch. Advait felt that he should go to drop them off as there were five of them in their car. He asked Saher and Shivani to come in his car. Advait spoke to Saher as at home he didn't get the opportunity to talk to him. All three of them spoke on various topics. Even after reaching Saher's home, their conversation continued for quite some time. As Advait was leaving he promised to show them the city.

Later, Advait and Ivanka took Saher and Shivani to all important places and briefed them about its history and culture.

After three days when Advait and Ivanka reached home, they were welcomed by a worried look of their parents. Advait thought that maybe they have said no to Ivanka and the thought worried him. Later he came to know that they have put a clause to the marriage of Ivanka and Saher. The clause was that they wanted

Shivani and Advait to be married too. Advait was devastated but such a good proposal for Ivanka was once in a lifetime one.

Advait was upset with his name being dragged in between. He realised that he being nice to Shivani was the cause of it as she had started to like him. He realised that she had mentioned it in the passing, but he had not given much attention to it. She must have concluded that his silence on the matter was his approval. Ivanka started crying a lot as she had fallen in love with Saher and she was sure that he was the one.

Things were getting complicated and Advait couldn't find any solution on the matter. To makes things worse, Saher and Shivani had a return flight back to Europe soon and hence the answer was to be given to them. They wanted to get engaged immediately. Ivanka took matters into her own hands. She informed Advait that if he didn't agree she would commit suicide and he will be responsible for it!

Advait suddenly realised that he had not updated Aadhya on the recent developments in his life! He rang her up and asked her to meet him. Aadhya was excited to meet him and informed him that she wanted to deliver some good news in person. She had got a job in Bangalore and she knew that she would definitely take it.

But when Advait finished narrating Aadhya the complete sequence of events, all Aadhya could do was to look at him in shock. She gathered herself and asked him what he had decided. Advait was quiet and Aadhya realised that he had made up his mind and he was now feeling sorry for her.

It was the guilt that was eating him up from inside. So she knew that she will have to take the initiative. She held Advait's hand and told him that he has to sacrifice his love for his family. As soon as she said it, Advait started crying and shook his head trying to tell her no. She held his head in her hand and told him, "Listen, love does not mean that we become selfish. Love means sacrifice. Here we need to sacrifice our love itself, which is the highest form of love!"

"Just think, how many people get such an opportunity to sacrifice their love?" She started wiping his tears. She continued,

"You need to be brave. Your sister's life and family's wishes and reputation is at stake. Please don't be selfish. See the larger picture not just your wishes. Goodbye!" Saying this she walked away neither hugging him nor looking at him. She was crying and she didn't want him to see it. It would break him and he would not be able to accept reality. Adhya switched off her mobile. She had come expecting to shock Advait but ended up being shocked herself.

Advait & Shivani got married and left for Europe as they both were offered a job in a multinational company, while Adhya commenced with her new job in Bangalore.

Six months later, Adhya was informed that a client is coming from Europe. In the conference room she was sitting at the edge of the table near the door as she was pregnant. To her surprise, it was Advait! He entered the room and her heart skipped a beat. Everyone stood up. After the guest and the manager sat down, everyone sat down.

Aadhya felt the child kick her and she was taken aback. She was happy and her mind took her to the future and her holding her child. The child seemed to have sensed the vibes of its father right in front, and in its excitement kicked from the womb.

EXECUTIVE DIRECTOR

"Compassion isn't about solutions. It's about giving all the love that you've got."

– Cheryl Strayed

Anshu worked in a multinational company. She was very competitive but very kind-hearted at the same time. Her rise was phenomenal; a lot of hard work and good timely decisions were behind it. After joining as a Marketing Executive, she went on to become the Media & Marketing Manager. She had to coordinate not only with her team but also with the Accounts and Sales heads. Although powerful, she was easily approachable.

The managers had a separate section in the cafeteria. So, most of them met during lunch time. Only during the festivities time there would be very few of them. Accounts & HR Managers were very close to each other. Media & Marketing and Sales were close as their work needed each other.

The Sales Department was headed by Hriday— a family man, with a wife and young daughter. Anshu noticed that recently Hriday was missing from the office. She initially thought that he must have gone on vacation but on enquiring she came to know that he had been working from home.

Anshu rang up Hriday to enquire the reason and was shocked to learn that his wife had fourth stage cancer, and she had six more months only. Anshu felt sad for him. Out of curiosity, she asked if she could be of any help. Hriday said, "I have been working from home so that I can manage my work, my wife and attend to my daughter too."

Anshu said, "Please let me know if I can help in anyway."

Anshu sat in her home, facing the French windows, alone and sipped a drink. She thought of Hriday and how difficult it must be for him. She remembered her past. As soon as she had joined this company, she had got married. The very next year she delivered a healthy baby boy. He was the darling of the family and extended families. They regularly went on road trips. Her husband loved to drive, she would take the wheels from him in turns, so that he could rest. They were having the best time of their lives.

On one such trip, as they were driving through the mountains, a boulder rolled from the top and crashed on the adjacent truck! With the force of the impact, the truck rammed against their car. Her husband and child died on the spot. She suffered a lot of injuries but luckily survived. Being a positive person, she always tries to find out why she survived. That question was always on top of her mind. This question pushed her to help others as much as possible. She never found out the answer to her question. As she finished her drink and was ready to go to sleep, she decided that she must go to Hriday's home after work and see if she can be of any help.

After work, Anshu went to Hriday's home to meet him. When she reached there, she found out that Hriday was helping his daughter Heena with her homework. She apologized for coming unannounced. Hriday said, "Don't stress it's okay. At least you came. I am happy. You relax till I finish this math problem with her." There was a bell and Hriday got up to go inside.

Heena frustratingly complained, "Every day this happens, and my homework does not complete and teacher gets upset."

Anshu asked Heena, "May I help you with your homework?"

Heena smiled and said, "Yes, please help me."

Anshu helped Heena solve her math problem and also finished her pending homework. Hriday came in between once but Anshu gestured to him to be with his wife.

Then Anshu got up to leave and Heena said, "Thank you. You are better than Daddy as you did not scold me when I made mistake!"

Anshu patted Heena's back and said, "Should I come daily and help you in your homework?" There was a big smile on Heena's face and excitingly she hugged Anshu and said, "Yes, please, please come!" Anshu left happy. As soon as she sat in the car, tears rolled down her cheeks. It had been more than three years since she got a hug from a child. She visualized her son. It was something that she would never forget in her life.

Going to Hriday's house became a daily routine. Initially Hriday would sit but then Anshu suggested to him to be with his wife as that was where he is needed the most. Four months later, Hriday's wife passed away. Heena was sobbing uncontrollably. Anshu took her in her arms and tried to pacify her. The next few days, Hriday was busy, so Anshu took the responsibility of Heena. She left only after putting Heena to sleep.

This became a daily routine for the next few months. After making Heena sleep, she would spend some time with Hriday. He was sad but at the same time grateful to Anshu for taking care Heena so lovingly. He said, "You have helped Heena overcome her sadness. She misses her mother but overall, she is has returned to normalcy. I am eternally grateful to you for the love and care. After being under your wings, she is doing far better in her studies than before. Thank you."

Anshu felt awkward and said, "Please don't say such things. I am glad that you gave me this opportunity as she has healed my hurting heart. I think she came as a blessing for me. Take good care of her as she is a lovely child."

Hriday said, "I heard about what happened to your family. You are a lady with a big heart. You making space for my daughter in your heart itself is a great gesture! I wonder how you overcame your grief. I can't come to terms with mine." Saying this Hriday started to cry.

Anshu wiped his tears and gave him a tight hug. She knew he needed it as much as Heena. As Anshu drove home, she thought how difficult it must have been to see your loved ones die a slow death. Six months of torture in his mind. Sad part was he couldn't show it as he had to take care of his wife and daughter. The emotions were now welling up. Since that day, she started to take care of Hriday and Heena.

One day, Hriday was really sad and feeling very lonely; so, he requested Anshu to wait after putting Heena to bed. He was crying, talking about his wife, her suffering. Anshu sat next to him and tried to console him. She wiped his tears and hugged him. She made a drink. It made him sadder as everything in the house had a memory attached to her. So, Anshu provided him with more drinks. This helped him and he started to feel sleepy.

She helped him go to his bedroom and made him sleep but he never let go of her. He pulled her next to him in his sleep. She slowly but steadily started to withdraw from his grip. Before she could realise, he kissed her all over her face. He kept repeating his wife's name saying, "I miss you so much." Slowly she wriggled out of his grip and tidied herself before heading home. In the car, she remembered that it has been more than three years since a man had touched her and kissed her. She was surprised that there was no remorse nor guilt in her heart. She felt good and then it dawned on her that she had fallen in love with him! She decided not to tell him.

One month had passed after the incident; Hriday started to feel lighter and better. Anshu's presence in his house made a huge difference. His attention was more on Anshu and less about his wife's memories. Anshu was happy that he had overcome his grief, but she knew that a trace of sadness would always remain in his heart. The pain would be very minimal. After putting Heena to sleep, Anshu came and sat near Hriday every day. He spoke now on various topics under the sun. They enjoyed their drinks and she left.

One day Hriday said, "Since you came into our life, there has been drastic change for the good. We were able to come back to normal so soon. You have filled Heena's life and heart with love. I don't know if it's appropriate or not, but I think we should be together. I feel that we are meant to be together. Just think, if I had not opted for work from home then you might not have come in our lives. On that day, when you had come, if my wife wouldn't have called out to me, then you might have not come again. Everything that happened was for you to be part of us!"

Anshu interrupted, "What are you trying to say?"

Hriday continued, "I feel that you should be here. I can't ask you to marry me for two reasons. Firstly, I want at least one year to pass. Secondly, I need Heena's opinion. I can tell you one thing, I really love you from the bottom of my heart."

Anshu went up to Hriday and hugged him. They both kissed each other passionately. Anshu said, "Let's give each other and Heena some time and then let's take it up from there."

In the office, there came an opening for an Executive Director. Two names were shortlisted: One was Anshu —Marketing Manager and the other was the Accounts Manager. Opinion was sought of everyone as to who was better suited for the job. Hriday unbiasedly thought that Accounts Manger would be better for the job. Anshu later was told that it was a close competition, and she lost by just one vote. She somehow managed to get hold of the confidential list to find out whose vote tipped the scales against her.

To her surprise and shock, it was Hriday! She was upset. When she reached Hriday's home, she ignored him and concentrated on Heena and her studies. All this while, Hriday was wondering what had gone wrong.

After putting Heena to sleep, she came out of the room shouting, "Because of you, I have not become Executive Director. The Chairman had assured me that if there is a tie then his vote goes to me."

Hriday gave his reasoning, "I voted for Accounts not because I didn't want you to be the Executive Director, but because

Accounts person as a Director will be able to control expenses of every department. This will bring progress and profit to the company."

Anshu screamed, "You think I couldn't do it?"

Just then, she felt little fingers were holding her hand. All her anger melted when she saw Heena who for the first time addressed her as, "Mother what happened?"

Anshu started crying and said, "Nothing my child." Then Anshu hugged her and lifted her in her arms and started to kiss her all over her face she again became a mother. A mother was born within her and all her grudge melted away instantly.

CREATOR

"If you are rooted in that dimension which is the source of creation; if one part of you is creator, another part of you is creation, you can play with creation whichever way you want, but it will not leave a single scratch upon you."

-Sadhguru

Randeep received an email which had an invitation to a debate. The topic of the debate was, "Did God create Man or did Man created God?" He was a spiritual person and had often spoken on spirituality and science. He sat wondering how he would prepare himself for such a discussion. He replied, "I am honoured and humbled having being selected amongst such an eminent panel of speakers. I accept the invitation only on one condition that I will speak after all other speakers finish their talks."

A few days later, he received acceptance to his condition along with the schedule. Randeep read a lot of scientific articles as well as religious articles on the subject. He was not sure whose side he should speak, as both sides, religious and science had no concrete evidence of how the world was created. Randeep felt that only once this is established then the question of who created whom could be arrived at. The dilemma was like answering if the chicken came first or the egg.

The day of the debate arrived. The auditorium was full. There were only a few interested journalists and video recording of the event was arranged. On the dais, arrangements were made for seating of one Hindu, one Muslim and one Christian speaker. After that were the three scientists seats and at the far end was Randeep's seat. One of the scientists was known to Randeep who was waiting in the aisle of the stage.

As soon as the scientists arrived on the stage, Randeep joined them. It was clear that he wanted the scientists whom he knew to seat next to him. The names in front of the seats had already been placed earlier. Seeing this, he requested the scientists to exchange the plaque. One of the volunteers rushed and helped.

The debate started with the Hindu who said "The Universe manifested from the body of Maha Vishnu. Every time he exhales, infinite universes get created from the pores of his divine body. And when he inhales, all universes get sucked in again. Hence God created Man!"

The scientists who spoke said, "It's nothing but the description of the black hole theory! This could be a later addition to the scriptures."

The Muslim speaker said, "I want to quote a beautifully written verse by Galib, *"Na that kuch tho Kudha tha, Kuch na hoga tho Kudha hoga"*. Even before modern science existed, Kudha existed and is beyond time. Hence God created Man."

The next scientist said, "Scriptures are a last few thousand years old. The Universe is far beyond that. The origin of the Universe varies in each religion."

The Christian speaker said, "In the Bible, it is very clear that the first inhabitants of species on Earth were humans. We are all descendants of Adam and Eve. Hence God created Man."

The last scientist said, "Man created God for seeking external help. In fact, I will go one step further and say, man needed someone to blame. Hence, he created God in heaven. Otherwise, tell me how the scriptures that discuss the creation of the universe could have missed the Stone Age, the Ice Age, and even the dinosaurs? It just proves my point!"

Finally, it was the turn of Randeep. He said, "Basic elements create - period. The water creates rivers, ponds and seas. Without water they can't exist. Similarly, man has created God for his emotional and spiritual growth. God has also created man like how the water creates. The way to summarize this whole debate would be that without each other, none can survive. It will be very fair to say that when God and Man met both exclaimed, "My Creator!" There is no existence without each other."

GOING WITH THE FLOW

"Life is like a river. The way of life is to flow with the current. To turn against it takes effort but the current will carry you if you let it. Float with joy and ease."

- Anonymous

Aarya was the guest speaker at a seminar. The hall was full of students who were going to graduate and going to merge in some industry to make a career for themselves. He knew the struggle they are to face as he too had passed through this phase to be where he is today. As he was invited to speak, he got up and went to the podium. Today he didn't carry any notes.

Aarya started his talk with, "Many years ago, I was seated where you'll are today. Then, I heard a professor speak and was influenced by his idea of speaking ex-tempo. Hence today, I too will be doing the same. I will try to recall from my memory, the talk that changed my life. I sincerely hope it changes yours too!" Aarya took a pause and looked around to see many eager faces. They looked as if they were ready to grasp what he was about to reveal to them. He continued, "The professor said that if you really want success then do what others do not dare to do."

"This lesson remained with me all my life. It continues to inspire me even today. A lot of people think that it's unconventional or hard way of achieving success. I don't think so, as every path that you take up has its own challenges. We have to overcome them if we want to go to the top. That is how every path is designed."

"Swimming against the tide might be more difficult than swimming with the tide. Let me assure you, that swimming with the tide makes you one of the many but swimming against the tide makes you one of a kind. It builds your character to face everything that life throws at you. Your will power increases as well as your determination. You will always be strong during crises."

"Swimming against the tide also teaches you to stand up for yourself as well as stand with and for others." Aarya took another pause and let his words sink in the students. This time he took a longer pause to give the impression that he is thinking. Aarya continued, "Leaders and innovators are the ones who swim against the tide. People who make a mark in other peoples' lives are the ones who have not followed the oft- trodden path but chalked out new paths for themselves and for others to follow."

"You may not have a map or guidance, but you will have to trust your beliefs and confidently move ahead. Like I said earlier, that every path has its challenges. If it's a smooth path then remember that you are either lucky or the path will not take you far towards the road to success. This is actually the most preferred path to many. It is well known and well-travelled. Most of the challenges have precedent and hence ready-made solutions are available. I also know that most of you will choose it not because you are afraid of challenges but because of peer pressure or society pressure that you will face."

"For many it's the only path available due to their situation and where life has placed them. Few of you, I think one will be able to count on the fingertips, the ones who will take the path of the unknown. Years later, one among you will be standing here and speaking to the future generation of students and telling about your success story. That is how the cycle of life works. Every generation produces few inspiring personalities to inspire and guide the future generation."

"I wish to take up this opportunity to inform you'll that I am available to give guidance to you'll whichever path you choose to take. The Principal Sir has my number and email address. Thank you for your patient hearing." There was a thunderous applause as everyone in the dais and the audience gave him a standing ovation. It was a heartwarming homecoming for Aarya to be back in his college after so many years. The Principal took his hand and lifted it towards the crowd as he guided Aarya towards his seat.

After the felicitation, Aarya preferred mingling with the students on his way out. He was stopped at every step for autograph and or selfie. Only one student stopped him and said, "Sir, I want to be like you." He shook hand with that boy and gave him a hug and said, "You will be better than me." The boy was beaming from ear to ear. Aarya sat in his car and drove off. His mind was not on the road. He was in auto drive mode. His mind was on the talk he just gave.

He was pleased that he inspired at least one student to swim against the tide. Suddenly he heard a lot of honking. He realized that he had entered a one-way street from the opposite direction. He started laughing at himself thinking he was physically going against the tide! Just then he saw a constable indicating him to park his car on the side. Before he could say anything, the constable handed him over the challan and said, "What do you think, you will go against the tide and I shall allow you?".

ADD FRIENDS

"The most important discovery true friends make is that they can grow separately without growing apart."

- Elisabeth Foley

Rakesh, Suresh and Kartik were classmates for a few years now. They had met in the 7th standard. Now their schooling was coming to an end, in one month. The pressure of the final Board Exams eclipsed the fact that they might not meet again. Each of them had a separate centre to write their exams. Meeting was not possible, but they decided that on the last day they would all meet.

They met in a restaurant and discussed how they fared and what percentage they would get. They also discussed their future course which they would be opting. Eventually, each one joined different branches of study: Rakesh joined to become a doctor, Suresh joined Accounts and Kartik joined Arts. Thus, each one drifted from each other.

Dr. Rakesh finished his MBBS and then was called by a relative to the US; he had to do his MD (US MBBS) all over again, as Indian degree was not accepted there. As years rolled by, he specialised as a heart specialist. Workload kept him busy, so he came to India only when absolutely necessary. He married a girl from the Indian community in the US.

They had two children. How years rolled by, he just didn't understand until he received an email from Kartik. It was an invitation to the alumni of his classmates called, "Batch of 1984" from his school. He saw the school days roll in front of him as he read the email. He remembered his best friends Suresh and Kartik and wondered what they were upto.

Suresh had completed his B. Com and had specialised in Financial Cost Accountancy. He went on to work in a multinational company for three years before joining his father. After joining his father, he applied all the learnings of the multinational company in his father's firm and took it to new heights. His father, seeing his success, slowly handed over the company to him. Suresh married in his community as per the selection of his parents.

It was also a mutual benefiting proposal, as his father-in-law was one of the leading component manufacturers. Suresh had only one child – a boy. There were two miscarriages and hence they did not pursue to have another child. The trauma left a scar in Suresh and his wife's heart. Time is the best healer and so the entire attention was focused on his son and his business. Years rolled by and one day he received an email from Kartik. It was an invitation to the alumni of his classmates called, "Batch of 1984" from his school.

He remembered his best friends Rakesh and Kartik and wondered where they were placed in life. He was surprised and found it strange that none of them had made any effort to meet. The invitation was a refreshing way to go back to their school days.

Kartik had completed his Bachelors in Arts with specialisation in Philosophy. During his college days, he joined the theatre and did some plays. Later he wrote and directed some plays too. The topic was mainly philosophy of ancient India. He felt that there was no representation of this rich cultural heritage. He was dubbed as a flop writer and director. Very few people were ready to invest in such theatrical venture.

He started to act in small roles to meet his expenses. He was not interested in acting. It was just a means of survival. He always dreamt of having to direct a Broadway kind of show. He was confident that he would be successful at it. His luck turned when NMACC started in BKC. Theatre owners were suddenly worried and at this time he pitched his play called, "Durga" to the Prithvi Theatre Manager.

The manager sought the permission of the Management as it was a very big change in the way they functioned. This involved the best of choreographers, digital imaging, set designers, costume designers and numerous artisans apart from singers, musicians and actors. Luckily the Management agreed but with conditions that the best person in each field to be selected by them. Specialists from Kolkata were called to give it the authentic touch.

This was tipped to be the best extravaganza of the century. Some called it the Broadway of India. Karthik's dream was fulfilled, way more than what he could envisage. Beyond his wildest dreams. It was an opportunity of a lifetime; in fact, it was history in the making. The first show was full of invites. The who's who from every field were present. It was a grand success. Karthik was suddenly the talk of the town. Documentaries were made but he knew that it was a team effort. He acknowledged the top heads of each section. He also mentioned that without their support this was not possible.

One day, he got a call from his school principal requesting him to come and meet. The Principal was new, but someone had told him that Karthik had studied here. The Principal suggested that he try to contact his classmates for a meeting. Suresh suggested the name, "Batch of 1984". The school researched and got numbers and email addresses of most students.

The day of the get-together arrived for the Batch of 1984. It was a home coming for most of the students. Nostalgic memories and reintroduction to each other was in progress. Most of them were beyond recognition as they looked completely different. Few women had managed to maintain their looks and figures. Suresh, Rakesh and Kartik met each other and were very happy. They updated themselves about each other. An announcement, interrupted their conversation, requesting Suresh to come on the dais.

Suresh joined a few who sat on the Dias. The Principal welcomed them and thanked them for coming in spite of their busy routine. After the Principal's speech, a cultural program was arranged. Suresh invited Kartik and Rakesh to sit with him in the front row along with the Principal. After the cultural function, it was the turn of Suresh to give the vote of thanks. Suresh said, "Principal Sir has already welcomed you'll and has left me with to say goodbye to all of you."

There was laughter and after the laughter died down Suresh continued, "I am sure it has been great fun for each and every one of you, as it is for me, to meet our classmates and friends once again after a gap of over thirty five years. This for me is a very emotional moment, not because I have been a small part of the organising committee, but because I can physically see each and every one of you. Our friends and classmates share so many memories which were lost in our pursuit towards achieving our dreams, our lives and building a family life.

I need to thank the Principal on two counts, firstly for coming up with this idea and secondly for thinking that I am capable enough to be part of this. Nowadays things have changed so much that all our communication is digital not physical. I want to end by saying that nowadays we don't make friends anymore. We just add them nowadays." There was a standing ovation with everyone clapping. The thought resonated in everyone's heart.

MOTHER @ 50

"The loveliest masterpiece of the heart of God is the heart of a mother."

-St. Therese of Lisieux

My name is Kavita and I have delivered a baby boy recently. For all, it is an embarrassment as I am fifty years old. Let me tell you my life story; you might find it interesting!

I married my childhood sweetheart, Pravin, at the age of twenty-three. The thing is that, since school we were together and then our friendship turned into love. We were staying in the same society and studied in the same school and in the same class. Pravin was only a few months elder to me. Our parents were friends too and hence we used to visit each other's homes. We used to study till late night in each other's house. Those days we were innocent and hence we actually studied. Both got good marks. I branched into Accounting whereas Pravin went into Engineering. This reduced our joint studies.

One day, when I went to their house Pravin was alone at home. I had forgotten that they were to go to attend a marriage. We discussed about each other's college and academics, the difference between school and college, etc.

Suddenly out of the blue, Pravin held my hand. I felt it was not the regular touch. I didn't flinch nor felt odd. It was as if it was a natural movement in our relationship. Pravin was nervous and I could feel his hands trembling. I knew exactly what he was feeling as the same feeling was within me for quite some time. I missed him and had the urge to meet him. Maybe that's why, unknowingly I landed in his house today. It was as if the Divine had planned this. I tried to calm his trembling, but it only increased. I am sure he wanted to hold my hand since long; he must have mentally rehearsed it.

Yet, the soft skin of my hand when he touched it, sent vibrations through his body. I was enjoying it but not showing it. I had to act my part as he had taken the initiative. Somehow after about five to ten minutes he steadied himself and said sheepishly that he loved me. When he said it, I felt very different from what I thought I would feel. It suddenly made me shrink! It was an involuntary reaction to the touch. I knew he must have become more nervous, so I looked up and our eyes met. He lowered his eyes out of guilt.

I held his hands in mine and started to rub his hand with my thumb. His body suddenly shrugged violently. I thought he might fall, so held his shoulder with the other hand. Another wave of shiver went through his body. All the initiatives were taken by me. I smiled and asked what he wanted to say. He was now in a better shape and appeared confident. He looked at me sheepishly and said that he loved me. I said that I loved him too. That suddenly must have stirred his groins. He held both my hands and hugged me. He wrapped his hands on my back. I too took the opportunity and wrapped my hands around his. We had hugged each other before so it was not anything special. Yet, there was a big difference in this hug. We hugged like lovers and hence it lasted much longer.

His confidence seemed to increase, as now his hands started to rub my back. I allowed him to do it for some time. It suddenly struck me that no one was at home. He could take advantage of the situation, so I withdrew myself from the hug. I sat down and gestured him to sit. I saw that his confidence was doubling by the minute. I was glad that I withdrew. He started to gently caress my hair. I saw him and it felt that the Pravin I knew had grown up right in front of me, in that very moment!

He then began to caress my face. I knew things were going out of hand and I did not want to encourage him. So, I stood up and said that its dinner time and my parents must be waiting. I asked if he would join us. He said that his mother had prepared for him. I began to walk towards the door when suddenly he pulled me for another hug. This time, I put my both hands on his chest as to have buffer space. I did not want him to take things so fast. He looked puzzled and asked me, "Why? What happened between two minutes ago and now?"

I replied, "Love should grow from a tiny bud to a beautiful flower. Let's take small steps. I fully trust you, but I want our love to last till we are seventy to eighty years old. The love and excitement that I feel now, I want it to last till our lifetime! You think I am not excited? My heart is pounding like crazy! I trust you so much that I can surrender myself completely to you."

"Normal couples fall in love when their hormones start tickling. We are not like them. We have grown up together and our love is the result of our long relationship. We may have confessed to each other today. You know and so do I, that we were always in love. Like how we enjoyed our innocent childhood being together, same way let us enjoy our youth being together as both as lovers and friends! We are friends first and then lovers."

I opened the door and was leaving when I heard Pravin say, "Why do you think so much?"

I replied, "I am a girl and all girls need to think."

We continued seeing each other and after college we used to go to see movies. He would inevitably book back row corner seats in empty theatres. He knew which film had flopped and would take me there only. The first two movies were just kisses and holding hands and catching up with each other's life. Slowly his arm was around my shoulder and his fingers were probing my body. He got bolder and bolder. He ran his hand all over my body. I knew where to draw the line, but he was getting desperate. I could see that he wanted me completely which was not possible in a theatre.

I too was losing my grip over myself. I told myself that he is a man, so he needs it. The conflict and struggle between my mind and my heart went on. But somehow I managed to calm his urges in the dark theatre and let the moment pass.

He had applied for hostel room at the start of the year but was not allotted, as outstation students were given priority. One room had become vacant, and Pravin was asked if he would take it. Pravin gladly accepted it. Now he would have the freedom to meet me whenever he wanted!

Girls were not allowed in the boy's hostel. Pravin learnt that the warden would not be available on a particular day due to some official work.

He planned my arrival perfectly, at a time when the hostel was nearly empty. We went to his room which he locked. He was in a hurry to have sex immediately. I told him to chill. Take it easy. I reminded him, "Don't you remember from bud to flower?"

"Not now, please." he pleaded.

"You got protection?" I asked.

He nodded.

"First let's sit and then slowly move ahead…".

He did not even wait for me to complete my sentence. His lips locked around mine. Our bodies were heating up. I too couldn't help myself. Then we did it slowly at the beginning but then we both lost our patience.

The memory was a very good one because we broke rules of the hostel to have our first sex! We talked about our future. We planned that day the entire schedule of events that will take place in our lives. There was not an iota of doubt in our minds.

By the time Pravin finished his engineering I was already working. After the first one, we had sex only two times in 4 years. Lack of opportunities and exams tension all added up.

Pravin was picked up in the campus placement. Our parents got to know through our helpful but jealous neighbours about our love affair. Once it became official, we visited each other's homes and would meet after work or after dinner. We snatched moments to kiss each other in the lift or on the terrace. After one year of service, Pravin's parents thought that he was settled. So, they came home and asked my parents to fix a date for the marriage. Immediately the first thing that was done was, our engagement was arranged.

It was a small function with only his close relatives and our closed ones. In those days, in middle class families, engagement was a very personal and small function. Some photos were taken, and lunch was served. Both families mingled with each other, now not as neighbours but as in-laws. Main topic was always the date of the marriage, how many leaves would we get from work, how many people to call from each side, etc Last but not the least was the planning for the honeymoon.

The marriage went off very well.

The function and bending to catch the feet of so many elders exhausted us to no end. The excitement and buzz that was in the air kept us going. A hotel room was booked for our first night. We were excited and exhausted at the same time. The excitement was meeting some of the relatives after so long. Though the meeting was very brief, it pumped energy into us. For some time, we talked to each other about each other's relatives.

Then I went towards the mirror to take out my jewellery.

"Please don't take them out as yet. Let me see my bride in her beautiful best. The whole day there was never a chance to see you thoroughly. Let my eyes soak you up!" said Pravin as he gentle came towards me.

"Oh! So, now my husband is a poet? Engineer poet?" I teased.

We both laughed but I was pleased to the core. This is what I wanted. Togetherness and appreciation of each other.

He continued, "This is once in a lifetime opportunity. This moment will never come back again in our lives." Saying this, he turned me towards him. I was also soaking the glow on his face and the genuine love in his eyes. He seemed to understand and made me sit on the bed. He too sat facing me.

He said, "Today there is absolutely no hurry. I hope you don't mind if it's late and I know it already is."

I nodded as I could see a new matured Pravin in front of me.

In my mind the movie ran. I saw the little boy grow into a desperate youth to a matured man who sat in front of me. He kept soaking me up as if he wanted to etch my image in his mind forever.

I started to take out my earrings and other jewellery very slowly one by one. I deliberately slowed it down. His eyes were making a movie of this moment. I was living the moment through his eyes. Slowly but steadily one by one, the jewellery as well as clothes were taken off from each other's body. It was like a slow-motion movie. That night neither of us were in a hurry. We went with the flow. I felt that it was very pure. It was two souls merging into each other. We just melted into each other. This was the best day of my life. By the time we went to sleep it was 6.00 am!

We stuck to the plan we both had decided in the hostel room after our first sex. Our first child —a boy, was born when I was twenty-five. We both did well in our jobs. Then by twenty-seven, we had our second child — a girl. We had planned for their upbringing as well as for their education. Our boy finished his education and started working. As parents, we began searching a suitable girl for our son. He surprised us by saying that he had already found his future wife! We were very happy for him. He said that he needs one more year before committing to marriage. We both agreed to give him time.

Let me tell you, that we also stuck to our plans of our love life till old age. We were the only couple among our families and friends who were always with each other. Our sex life and love life were as it was after marriage. In spite of the years, our love for each other only increased. Every night we took time to be with each other to discuss our day and any other topic we felt it was worth telling each other. We had sex occasionally and it was tender and loving. Many a times it was spontaneous without protection, but nonetheless continued without it.

Our son's marriage was the hot topic for us, as parents. This brought a sense of buzz and excitement. Hence in this excitement, the frequency of our love making also increased, and that too usually without protection! Since we had crossed fifty, protection was not compulsory for us.

The day we met the girl and her parents, our excitement had skyrocketed. That night, after dinner, we reenacted our first night. I wore my jewellery as well as the best sari, complete with makeup etc. Pravin too wore his best suit and perfume. We soaked in each other completely. We made love very slowly and our body and soul nearly merged. Though age and circumstances had taken out the magic of the first night, it was the second best night of my life.

Two months later I fell sick. I took some medicine, but nothing worked. So, I went to see our family doctor. The doctor was surprised but did not tell me but asked for a retest. The results came same as before.

"You are pregnant. I don't know if I should congratulate you or not." the doctor, hesitantly told me.

"How?" I was shocked.

"How else do you think?" asked the doctor.

"I mean, I have crossed fifty! How can this happen?" I defended.

The doctor explained, "These things happen sometimes. There is a lot of risk both to you as well as the child. You and your husband need to think this through. You'll have grown up children. They will also have to be talked to, if you'll want to keep the child. Please first talk to your husband and let me know if you'll are going for abortion or not." Saying this she led me to the door.

I left and immediately rang up my husband and asked him to drop everything and come. He came and met me at our favourite restaurant. I knew talking at home could be dangerous if not disastrous. Such a sensitive topic considering that my son will be marrying and me delivering his sibling. There were other factors to be considered too. We also needed to know the opinion of our soon to be daughter-in-law. Our child should not break up our son's relationship.

Pravin came, we ordered coffee and sat facing the others so that we could spot immediately if anyone came close to us. I informed Pravin about my pregnancy. He was happy. I told him of the risk factors and the advice of the doctor. I told him what my feelings and concerns were in this matter. Now he was confused and lost.

Finally, he said, "So many things have to be taken into account just because you are pregnant? Why? Let it be simple!"

After all an engineer. He started to tackle the issue like a project. He made bullet points in his head.

Then he said, "First point to be considered is whether to go ahead considering the risk to you and the child. Let us take the first step. You want to go ahead with the pregnancy naturally as it's the labour of our love. But I have to consider the risk factor too. I love you and would always place you above everything else. Then, I also have to consider your likes. Have I ever gone against it ever? No I don't think so. Let me think so give me time to decide.

Now the second issue you raised was what the world will think. You know my answer: to hell with the world! Your other thought was what will our in-laws and relatives think? If they don't respect our sentiments, then why should we? We will know when we both take the decision.

Last but not the least, taking our children into confidence. Yes, we must but not because our son is getting married but because we need to respect their feelings not opinions."

He took a sip of his coffee and continued, "Now coming back to the first question. Both of us would never want to see either of us depart. Our love is very strong. So is our respect for each other and our wishes. This is the first time that we both have to decide what we choose. You know me, my answer has always been if your heart tells you then go ahead. For me it's the right decision. Now let's go home and call our children home too and break the news to them. We both have time to decide." We left for home and on the way, we called for an urgent family meeting.

When we broke the news to our children, their reaction was typical. How can you'll be so careless? At this age, you'll will have a child? It's our time not yours. Your time is to play with your grandchildren not your own.

It hurt, but Pravin had asked me to just keep quiet. He ensured it by squeezing my arm tightly. Pravin allowed them to vent out their frustration and shock. He let them cool down and then said, "Both sit down. I know and understand that the situation is not normal. Your reaction was typical. I just want you to consider this before you'll come to any conclusion.

This is not normal, but we feel our parenting lacked something. We taught and allowed you'll to have an open mind and gave you'll space as well as freedom. The one thing probably we missed teaching you was to respect others' decisions and feelings!

I just want you'll to look at this from our point of view. Also look at this way - don't we have the freedom to take our own decisions? Do we need the worlds or your in-laws or your permission in taking decisions that affect our lives first and foremost? The others come next including you.

I feel sad that both of you did not ask the right questions: What did the doctor say? What is the kind of risk involved? What's the percentage of success rate at this age?

Do you'll realize that both of you have been selfish? You'll are worried about being ridiculed by society. Not once your focus was on us. Can you imagine how much we both will be ridiculed? We will be the butt of all jokes! Don't you think we know all this? We live in this world and hence are aware what all can happen.

I called this meeting to inform you'll, not to be grilled by you'll. Just for your information, we have not yet decided on the matter. I feel sorry that I disturbed you'll from your work. Whenever and whatever we decide, we will inform you'll."

Pravin held my hand and walked away from them, towards our bedroom. Children tried to follow but Pravin gestured them not to.

The next morning, children came to the kitchen and said that they were so taken aback by the news that they didn't know how to react.

I told them, "It's okay now. I think you should talk to your fiancé and check with her how she feels and how her parents feel. I don't want to jeopardize your life. It is very essential that we keep this within our two families only. Your dad and I have not yet taken our final decision. Now take your breakfast and act normal. Nothing has happened as yet."

We all left for our work as usual. That evening, Pravin met me at the same restaurant. We had coffee together and I congratulated him on his strong lecture.

I told him, "You analyse things very well. I agree that children need to learn to respect others' opinions even when it is against theirs. Something like being gracious in defeat!"

He smiled and sipped his coffee. We left for home. On reaching home we saw our son with his fiancé. We exchanged greetings and pleasantries. Then as we sat down his fiancé spoke, "Uncle, I liked what you mentioned yesterday to your children. I liked your thought process and viewpoint."

She continued, "Most of us have looked up to you'll as the perfect love couple that has not been withered by time. In fact, I feel with every passing day, your love and bonding grew and became stronger. I am concerned about Aunty. I don't want to repeat what you must have heard from the doctor. So, I did my own research. There is not much data on mothers over fifty delivering a child in India. Abroad, there are and the health care system there takes special care of such mothers. I am not suggesting that you move abroad. If you'll decide to keep the child, then I would love to help. The similar care we can arrange here too!"

She added further, "Please let me know once you'll decide. To be honest, my parents' opinion is similar to your children's opinion. However, I assure you that I will turn them around!"

I got up and hugged my future daughter-in-law. I felt that the right girl was coming to our house. In this matter, my son had taken a right decision. That night, Pravin came and held my hand for a long time. Then kissed them. He placed them on his shoulders. He then hugged me. It was a long hug. I knew he wanted to make the moment a memory.

Whatever he had in his mind would come at the end. So, I waited patiently and went with the flow. He then held my face as if studying it. I looked at him in wonderment. He hugged me and I wrapped my hands around him. Time stood still as we continued hugging each other. He turned his face towards mine and whispered in my years. "We should have this child. Oh God! You look beautiful when you are pregnant." I blushed and gave him a kiss. He continued, "I missed the chance all these years. I should have made you pregnant every year and I could see you like this always."

I laughed and said, "I would have grown and looked old by 40 if it had happened!" We both laughed at it.

The next day morning, we announced our decision to our children. I called up our daughter-in-law and asked her to accompany Pravin and me to the doctor. The doctor seemed surprised by our decision but when our daughter in law told her what she had researched, the doctor reluctantly agreed. She also instructed us saying that at the slightest inconvenience we should come to her. She gave us the schedule for further checkups.

The date of delivery clashed with my son's wedding. So, I looked at my daughter-in-law. She smiled and said, "Mother this will be the best gift that I will receive. Trust me, even if you are unable to attend the wedding, I will arrange for you to see it. Technology today allows us to be anywhere and yet connected."

The doctor enquired, "Can't you'll prepone or postpone the dates of the wedding?" My daughter-in-law replied, "For a few days, yes, we can but the month we can't as that is the only time our jobs allow us to take leave. Otherwise, we will have to postpone it for a year!"

I told her, "Let's go home and discuss it with everyone concerned." She nodded her head in agreement. Everyone felt that the clashing of the two events couldn't be helped and hence allow it to happen. Though it was a reality but looked very funny, when a pregnant mother was giving invitation card of her son's wedding. Many laughed after we left, some giggled right in front of us looking at my stomach. This was to happen as the situation was abnormal. People can't digest abnormal happenings.

Two days before the wedding, I felt tremendous pain. I was rushed to the hospital and the doctor informed that there were some complications and hence the child had to be delivered by caesarean. I was rushed to the ICU. I saw them remove my baby girl through the monitor on the side panel monitor. By evening I was eager to know when I would be discharged. Doctor informed that no discharge before another two days. I knew I would miss my son's wedding. It couldn't be helped but the satisfaction was that all were present to welcome my sweet baby girl. My children with my daughter-in-law with her family.

My newborn baby girl is very lucky because so many people are there to love her. I felt overwhelmed just thinking of it. On the day of the wedding, I saw the entire ceremony through the hospital TV which my son had arranged. By the time I was discharged, it was 8.30 pm. When I reached home with my baby daughter, my son came with his wife. A fifty year old mother with her just born baby girl welcoming her twenty four year old son and his wife. What a sight it was to behold! It was a moment to be cherished for life.

HEAVEN

"You've gotta dance like there's nobody watching, Love like you'll never be hurt, Sing like there's nobody listening, And live like it's heaven on earth."

-William W. Purkey

Saransh was from a middle-class family. Saransh's family was very pious. They conducted prayer meetings and invited saints to their home.

Saransh finished his schooling and was leaving in a week to go to Rishikesh and stay in an ashram. One week later, Saransh left with his family to spend his holidays in Rishikesh. The ashram was like home for them. Most of the residents of the ashram knew them very well. They too knew most of them, much more than the people in their neighbourhood in Mumbai. They attended all the routines like, japas, meditation, pooja and satsangs held at the various places within the ashram. They rarely ventured out except for walks or to buy necessities.

One day, Swami Atma came to meet Saransh in his room. Saransh's parents had gone to see someone whom Saransh had already met. Hence, he opted out and stayed in the room. Swami Atma after the formality greetings started a discussion. They spoke on various topics, starting with Saransh's education and future. Then they spoke of the city and his family.

Saransh said, "I go to a school run by the brothers and fathers of the Christian community. They say that if one does good deeds then one is certainly going to heaven and if one does bad deeds then one certainly goes to hell. I am not sure if it is the same in other religions too."

Swami Atma said, "Yes it is the same. Muslims call heaven, Janat and we call it Swarg. Hell is called Narak in Hinduism and Muslims call it Jahannum. It is just different words, meaning the same thing. Let me tell you something interesting in our scriptures there are a lot of apparent contradictions. They are actually not contradictions but different schools of thought. We have the freedom to think differently. We may not agree with some of our famous scriptures."

Saransh looked surprised and asked, "Why is it so?"

Swami Atma replied, "We have different paths that ultimately leads to the same goal. It is there in other religions too, but they don't address it separately. They have merged all of them together. For example, you have seen in the ashram we all do japa. We have our japmalas with us. The Christians and the Muslims too have them. Christians call it rosary. Muslims call it Misbaha. Hinduism has given it a name for this practice. It is called Japa Yoga."

Saransh asked, "Just by repeating God's name, can one go to heaven?"

Swami Atma replied, "Certainly one can go to heaven. One can even go beyond heaven. Haven't you heard the story of Valmiki? By just repeating God's name, he became a Maharishi! He went on to write the great epic Ramayana!" He further added, "We have Dhyan Yoga, which is meditation. That too leads to heaven and beyond. Then there is also Gyan Yoga, in which one through knowledge and contemplation reaches heaven and beyond."

Swami Atma paused to see if Saransh was understanding it and then continued, "Same is the case with Karma or good deeds. In good deeds we go one step further we call it Nishkama Karma yoga. In this, expectation of the fruit of action is not there."

Saransh asked, "Everyone does something for a reason; hence it is considered as fruit isn't it? Please elaborate. One more thing I would like to know is, you keep referring to beyond heaven what is that?"

Swami Atma smiled as he clarified, "When we do an act with a particular reason behind it like to gain name, fame, wealth or even heaven, in the spiritual aspect of Hinduism it is termed as selfish. Whereas when one does a good deed without expectations then that deed is termed as selfless or Nishkama."

He continued, "Actually, it is our offering to God and feeling that I didn't do it, but it is God who did it through me. Hence, the fruits are not mine. This brings us closer to God who is in heaven. Now to your question of beyond heaven. Beyond all this earth, hell and heaven is God. God is the space where nothing exists. God fills everything and in everything is God."

Swamiji paused and said, "Just think, if God is in everything then where is heaven? If I may ask, is heaven everywhere? If heaven is everywhere so must be hell. Then are we living in hell or heaven? These are questions that very few people even consider, forget asking. I once heard a saint say that when your dad does a good work and gets a free holiday as bonus, then that is heaven. But when one is in a miserable state financially or with disease and is suffering then that is hell. Both heaven and hell are here only, on this earth! Our deeds decides whether we live in heaven or hell or we keep shifting between the two."

"It's like goings from one room to another. In summer if one room is air-conditioned and the other is not, then too it feels like heaven and hell."

Swami Atma then asked, "What if God meets you and asks you, 'So how was heaven?' What will you answer?"

A stunned Saransh just didn't know how to react or answer. He just looked with his mouth open as if he was frozen or shell shocked.

Swami Atma continued, "Heaven could be this earth. Do we want to create a heaven in our lives or hell depends upon you. We are the masters of our destiny. Ponder deeply over this as this will be the question you will need to answer all your life." Saying this Swami Atma left Saransh with this profound thought.

LAUGH AND LOVE

"When you awaken love and laughter in your life, your mind lets go of fear and anxiety, and your happy spirit becomes the healing balm that transforms every aspect of your human experience."

-Jesse Dylan

Long ago, there lived a princess, named Tanisha, who would not laugh. Nothing tickled her funny bones and that is why the King announced a handsome reward to the person who could make her laugh. People from all over the country came and tried their hand but nothing could make her laugh. The clowns and jesters all tried their best but in vain.

The King then extended the offer to the neighbouring kingdoms. The best clowns and jesters came and put up their best performance. To everyones' surprise no one succeeded in making the princess laugh! Though Tanisha had smiled at some of them, there was no laughter from her.

Later when she was back in her chambers, the ladies-in-waiting repeated the jokes and asked Tanisha why she didn't find it funny? Tanisha said, "It was good but not funny enough to laugh. I don't know why I don't feel like laughing. Though I did smile at them." The ladies were still laughing by repeating the jokes. Tanisha wondered what was so funny that these girls were still giggling.

A lady-in-waiting, Manisha, used to bring her son Parthiv along with her, since princess Tanisha was a small child. Parthiv was just one year elder to Tanisha. They bonded well but when Tanisha reached eight years of the age, the authorities asked Manisha not to bring Parthiv. It saddened both of them, but they knew that rules were meant to be obeyed.

Ever since the news of the King's challenge to make the princess laugh emerged, Parthiv has been pestering his mom to speak to the authorities about allowing him to be around the princess for a month. He was sure he could make her laugh. Manisha did not approach the authorities fearing losing her job. Parthiv thought that authorities would not heed to Manisha's proposal as she was working there, so he started to approach people close to the King.

Most of them did not take him seriously as they thought when professionals failed how could he make the princess laugh? A minister heard from his colleagues about Parthiv's claim. He thought, since everyone has failed, why not try him too as no one has succeeded till now. Also, there was no other option left. He took Parthiv to the King and convinced the King to allow Parthiv to try to make the princess laugh.

However, Parthiv said, "I have a few conditions. Firstly, I need one month with the princess alone."

Hearing this, the King jumped up from his seat. The minister gestured to the King to allow Parthiv to continue. Parthiv continued explaining himself, "This is because, I want the Princess to be comfortable with me. She has been under tremendous pressure to laugh." The King and the Minister nodded their heads in agreement.

"Also, once the princess trusts me, she will be able to give a hint on what tickles her funny bone. Most of the people, have already told all the jokes. My strategy will be do something foolish to bring out the laughter from her." said Parthiv.

The King got up and put his hand on the head of Parthiv, blessing him said, "You are the first person to explain this so beautifully. You are wise for your age. My best wishes and blessings for your success. I have one condition on you being alone with the princess. I want you to be with her in the garden or the lounge, but never in her chamber."

Parthiv nodded his head in agreement. Parthiv informed the King, "I would like to start from tomorrow."

Parthiv went and met his friends and family to inform them and take tips if any. Some suggested that he should run and fall in a very awkward way to make her laugh. Another suggested that he should make funny faces. After everyone left, one of his friends suggested to make her fall in love with him and she would be happy and thus laugh. He was not sure if any of these would work, as others had already tried them and failed.

Next morning, when he reached the palace, he was ushered to the garden. He sat on a bench and in front of him, 10 feet away, was a beautiful, comfortable and elegant seat kept for the princess. After a while Tanisha arrived, looked at him and went and sat in her seat.

She said, "Start!"

Parthiv looked surprised and said, "Start? What have you been told regarding why I am here?" Tanisha simply said, "To make me laugh!"

Parthiv said, "No! I have not come here to make you laugh. I told the King to try to understand how much pressure you have undergone. The expectations of everyone must have been awful. So, I asked the King to allow you to be free for a month. No one should try to make you laugh. That is my duty, only to set you free!"

Tanisha looked stunned, and asked, "The King allowed it?"

Parthiv nodded and smiled, "Hope you start to feel unburdened from the pressure you were feeling for such a long time."

Parthiv started understanding Tanisha by trying to make her speak about herself. He showed interest in knowing her likes and dislikes. Time seemed to fly when they sat and talked.

In a week, the princess, was now sure that Parthiv was there to keep the jokers out of her life. She started to paint and even write in the presence of Parthiv. King saw a change in her and was happy that she looked fresh. Parthiv started to tell her stories of people who were in love but failed. How some of them lost their lives because of love.

Tanisha asked Parthiv, "Why are you telling me sad stories, when you should be telling me happy stories? Don't you want me to be happy and laughing like everyone else?"

Parthiv was taken aback as this was the first time Tanisha had opened her heart and expressed a desire to laugh.

Parthiv replied, "I am sorry princess I did not know your likes and dislikes, so was just trying to understand you. Being happy or laughing is the easiest thing in the world! Yet, you can't, and I know you have tried but didn't succeed. Do you know why?"

Princess said, "I don't have any idea, that is why I asked you. I have never asked anyone but since I trust you, I asked you. As you said it's the easiest thing in life, but for me it's the most difficult one."

Parthiv said to the princess, "Do not stress. Please forget that you can't laugh. Your life is complete in every way. Since you want to laugh I can give you some suggestions, if you don't mind implementing them. Firstly, you have to be relaxed and be happy for others. This is the first step; the second step is to search for funny moments happening around you. You need not laugh but accept when they are funny. You may not treat others like yourself but at least be concerned about their lives. Ask them what brings them happiness. Be happy for them. For a child, a sweet may be the happiest moment of its life. What ticks for whom, you will need to understand."

This way, the princess started to search for happiness in and around her. In her life as well as in the life of others. In a few days, the princess began to feel happy.

Then one day, before the princess arrived in the royal garden, Parthiv had decided a new approach. As soon as Tanisha arrived she was ushered into her chair. Parthiv carried a very serious face. Tanisha enquired if everything was alright. Parthiv said that he had a challenge for her.

Parthiv said, “Lets play a game. I will narrate a story. But no matter how funny it gets, you should NOT laugh!I challenge you, you will lose!” Tanisha was puzzled and said, "Isn't it what I do daily?I will obviously win!" Parthiv said, "Wait and watch. Don’t laugh! This is serious!” He pulled out pictures from a folder.

It was a series of drawings of an elephant and an ant. Parthiv started pointing to the drawings. In one of them, an ant was looking up to an elephant and asking it to stop walking. The elephant stops and asks, “Why did you stop me?” The ant said, “We have our home here. Please take another route as our home will be crushed with your weight.” The elephant scoffed and told the ant to shoo away!

Tanisha was so engrossed in the story that she felt bad for the ants.

Parthiv noticed this and added emotion to his story telling. He described how the elephant ruthlessly crushed the ant hill. This saddened Tanisha very much. Her eyes were moist and face reflected her sadness. Then Parthiv described how the elephant mockingly sprayed water on their crushed home, trying to drown the surviving ants. The ant got angry and asked the other ants to gather a large leaf. Tanisha in surprise looked at Parthiv instead of the drawings. He drew her attention towards the drawings.

After the bath, the elephant picked up the leaf. Tanisha noticed that there were some ants on them. She pointed it to Parthiv who ignored her observation and continued his story. The next drawing was of the elephant consuming the leaf.

Parthiv drastically said that with the intention of taking revenge, the ants had purposefully sat on the leaf. As soon as the elephant picked up the leaf, the ants slid into the nostrils of the elephant and bit the insides so hard, that the elephant went crazy and started dancing!

Tanisha in her excitement and happiness started jumping and clapping. She was fully immersed in the story. She was now smiling and happy.

Parthiv continued the tempo and showed her drawings how the mighty elephant fell down and was turning and twisting. Suddenly she burst into a loud laughter, happy for the ants.

"Hey! Why are you laughing, Princess! You were NOT supposed to laugh, remember?!" teased Parthiv.

Tanisha was surprised hearing her own laughter.

Parthiv went and held her shoulders and said, "You know how to laugh but just forgot how to do it and how it sounds!"

Then suddenly, Parthiv tickled her. She laughed loudly till she had tears. The people in the palace who heard her laughter rushed to the King to give him this good news.

The princess was laughing and held Parthiv's hand and said, "Stop it. Before anyone comes, I want to tell you something." Hesitantly she put her face on his hand and kissed it. Parthiv was thrilled but also scared. The King might order his execution. He lifted the face of Tanisha and said, "You are a princess, and I am just an ordinary subject." The princess stopped him by putting her hand on his lips and hugged him.

They were in embrace when he remembered his friend's advice, "Make her fall in love to make her laugh." Parthiv thought, "Every time she laughs, I am the one who falls in love."

The King arrived and asked the princess to ask for a boon. The princess said that she would like to marry Parthiv. The King being a man of his word agreed.

---End---